Comprehension

The **READING PUZZLE**

Elaine K. McEwan
Michelle Judware
Darlene Carino
Candace Darling

CORWIN PRESS
Classroom

For information:

Corwin Press
A SAGE Company
2455 Teller Road
Thousand Oaks, California 91320
CorwinPress.com

SAGE, Ltd.
1 Oliver's Yard
55 City Road
London EC1Y 1SP
United Kingdom

SAGE India Pvt. Ltd.
B 1/I 1 Mohan Cooperative
Industrial Area
Mathura Road, New Delhi
India 110 044

SAGE Asia-Pacific Pvt. Ltd.
33 Pekin Street #02-01
Far East Square
Singapore 048763

Printed in the United States of America.

ISBN: 978-1-4129-5824-0

This book is printed on acid-free paper.

08 09 10 11 12 10 9 8 7 6 5 4 3 2 1

Executive Editor: Kathleen Hex
Managing Developmental Editor: Christine Hood
Editorial Assistant: Anne O'Dell
Developmental Writers: Michelle Judware, Darlene Carino, Candace Darling
Developmental Editor: Barbara Allman
Proofreader: Carrie Reiling
Art Director: Anthony D. Paular
Design Project Manager: Jeffrey Stith
Cover Designers: Michael Dubowe and Jeffrey Stith
Illustrator: Mark Mason
Design Consultant: The Development Source

TABLE OF CONTENTS

Introduction

The objective of reading instruction in grades K–3 is not only to enable students to read fluently and independently, but most importantly, to read with comprehension. By understanding what they have read, students are better able to remember, communicate, and apply the information they have gained through reading.

Developing reading comprehension also improves cognitive skills. Good readers think about what they read, and they are continually engaged in an ongoing dialogue with the text. Over time, reading extends their thinking. The structure and logic of written language enables the learner to more easily compose and grasp complex thoughts and meanings.

This book addresses the strategies that proficient readers need in order to unlock the meaning of written material. These strategies include:

- Activating prior knowledge

- Making connections

- Inferring

- Predicting

- Visualizing

- Questioning

- Monitoring and clarifying

- Searching and selecting

- Summarizing

Teaching cognitive strategies is vastly different from teaching "skills." Skills are procedures readers learn through repetition. Strategies tap higher-order thinking skills that will help students meet the demands of every unique reading task. Modeling these strategies for students is essential. The scaffolded approach of "I Do It," "We Do It," "You Do It" enables students to develop into successful, independent readers. Use these strategies along with other tools in this book, including graphic organizers, visual prompts, and activities, to engage and stimulate young readers.

Reading comprehension empowers students, giving them the ability to explore virtually any topic or subject in which they are interested. This book can help teachers instill the joy of reading, which, in turn, can lead to a lifetime of fulfillment and success.

 978-1-4129-5824-0

Put It Into Practice

An often repeated urban school myth states that many students are able to "word call" (i.e., nail the correct pronunciation of every word they encounter) but do not understand the meaning of what they read. Some say students are word callers because they had too much phonics instruction and too few opportunities to engage in meaningful literacy activities. This fallacy is often used to convince teachers not to waste time teaching decoding strategies when other compensating strategies (such as using context clues) will work just as well.

An in-depth study of 361 students in the early elementary grades examined various comprehension and decoding difficulties (Shankweiler et al., 1999). Students were tested on word and non-word reading, reading and listening comprehension, and language and cognitive ability. Those who did comparatively well at decoding, but whose comprehension was lower, were less common than students who were low in both decoding *and* comprehension. Low reading comprehension can occur in students with well-developed word-reading skills, but the most likely cause is ineffective instruction in vocabulary and reading comprehension strategies.

Cognitive strategies used to increase comprehension are an important piece of the Reading Puzzle. The Reading Puzzle is a way of organizing and understanding reading instruction, as introduced in my book, *Teach Them All to Read: Catching the Kids Who Fall Through the Cracks* (2002). The puzzle contains the essential reading skills that students need to master in order to become literate at every grade level. *The Reading Puzzle, Grades K–3* series focuses on five of these skills: Phonics, Phonemic Awareness, Fluency, Vocabulary, and Comprehension.

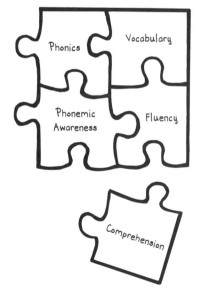

To describe what skilled readers do when they use cognitive strategies, I have coined the term *brain-based reading*. Brain-based reading is characterized by intentional action by the reader. It is the exact opposite what of some teachers laughingly call "brain-dead" reading, in which students simply stare at the page hoping for a cognitive miracle.

Cognitive strategies tap higher-order thinking skills in response to the demands of unique reading tasks. Strategies are used situationally. Students learn *how* and *when* to use cognitive strategies rather than "helping themselves" from a smorgasbord of content.

My vision for model instruction includes an extensive strategic reading program emphasizing four strategies with related permutations and combinations. These four strategies include: questioning, summarizing, organizing, and monitoring.

978-1-4129-5824-0

Students at every grade level must be shown how to use cognitive strategies through modeling; coached to proficiency through guided practice; and then expected to routinely explain, elaborate, or defend their positions or answers before, during, and after reading. When students are expected from the earliest grades to articulate explanations, they become accustomed to evaluating, integrating, and elaborating knowledge in new ways.

Questioning

Students should be the ones both asking the questions and then answering them, as well as replying to their classmates' questions. "Mind-reading" is a savvy questioning strategy. It looks something like this: Identify the most important ideas or concepts; process and manipulate the ideas into personal schema by using graphic organizers and summarizing the material; then pose questions to which one already has the answers. This kind of processing (rehearsal, review, comparing, contrasting, and making connections) increases the likelihood that students' newly acquired knowledge will be stored in long-term memory.

Summarizing

Summarizing can be described as getting the gist of what is read. Most students have difficulty summarizing what they have read. That is, unless they have seen the summarizing strategy modeled numerous times, been carefully taught the various aspects of the strategy, and then had the opportunity to practice in cooperative groups with teacher supervision—all before being expected to summarize on their own (Brown & Day, 1983; Brown, Day, & Jones, 1983).

Organizing

Organizing involves constructing graphic or visual representations that "help the learner to comprehend, summarize, and synthesize complex ideas in ways that, in many instances, surpass verbal statements" (Jones, Pierce, & Hunter, 1988/1989). By the time students enter high school, they should be able to construct various graphic organizers to help them understand what they read and organize their thoughts before writing (e.g., flowcharts, Venn diagrams, word webs, and so on).

Monitoring

Monitoring involves two related and often seemingly simultaneous abilities: thinking about how and what one is reading for the purposes of determining if one is comprehending the text, and using various strategies to aid in comprehension. Monitoring begins before the reader actually reads any text and continues long after the reader has finished reading.

CHAPTER 1

Oh, the Hats We Wear

As teachers, we all wear many different hats while we are at work. First and foremost, we teach grade-level content, but at any given time during the day, we might quickly "change hats" in order to become a nurse, parent, friend, social worker, or coach. The same idea applies to good readers. A good reader wears many different hats in order to get the most from written text. Good readers are actively engaged while reading a text. They have a clear and concise purpose, monitor their comprehension, and use a variety of strategies to fix problems in their understanding.

In this section, each reading strategy has a visual representation, or "strategy hat." See the **Hats Off! A Reading Strategy Guide reproducible (page 9)**. Each strategy hat can be clearly linked to a concept that will activate students' prior knowledge while engaging them in the text. For example, a police officer's duties involve generating, asking, and answering questions. Therefore, as students are reading, a police officer's hat will provide a visual clue to remind them that they need to continually use the reading comprehension strategy of questioning as they read the text.

Reading Strategy Hats

Strategy Bulletin Board (I Do It)

Create an interactive bulletin board in your classroom so you can refer to it as you introduce and model how to use the reading strategy hats. Photocopy the **Strategy Hats reproducibles (pages 10–18)** and use them to make a creative display.

As you introduce and model each new strategy, wear that strategy hat. Again, reproduce the Strategy Hats reproducibles or purchase hats rather inexpensively from a novelty store or catalog. While reading a story aloud, stop at the conclusion of each page or at a predetermined part of the text. Then, referring to the hat, model the use of the strategy. After modeling the strategy during a couple of sessions, reproduce the same strategy hat for students to decorate and wear. As you read aloud to the class, encourage students to take over the class discussion and become actively engaged in the text while demonstrating their ability to use the strategy.

Reading Strategy Cards (We Do It)

After you have introduced and modeled each strategy hat, photocopy, laminate, and cut out the **Reading Strategy Cards (pages 19–27)**. Randomly distribute them to several students before you read aloud to the class. Throughout the read-aloud session, the students holding the Reading Strategy Cards should show their understanding of the comprehension strategy by raising their card and explaining how it relates to the text being read. For example, if a student with the questioning strategy card (police officer hat) has a question concerning the text, he or she holds up the card and asks a question. This will indicate to you whether the student understands the strategy as well as the text. Using the Reading Strategy Cards during read-aloud sessions is an excellent way to model and practice having conversations with the text. To give everyone an opportunity to interact with the text, use more than one type of Reading Strategy Card at a time. Have students pass the cards on to others after they have used them.

Reading Strategy Bookmarks (You Do It)

Once you have modeled the strategies and students have had guided practice using the Reading Strategy Cards, introduce the **Reading Strategy Bookmarks (pages 28–36)**. Each strategy hat has a matching set of three bookmarks that you can use to prompt students' thinking and to actively engage them with text. These bookmarks serve as a way for students to guide their own textual discussions. Reproduce sets of the Reading Strategy Bookmarks, cut them out, and place them in baskets or folders for use during independent reading, partner reading, or guided reading groups. The bookmarks may also be hole-punched and placed on a ring for easy access and organization. (Place each set of bookmarks on its own ring.) Once students have had several opportunities to apply a bookmark's strategy as they read, introduce a new set of bookmarks.

After students have become proficient in using all of the strategies, introduce the **Strategic Thinker Bookmarks (page 37)**. Remove the individual Reading Strategy Bookmarks in order to further move students toward becoming independent readers who monitor their own comprehension. Prepare a basket of Strategic Thinker Bookmarks where it is accessible for students. Encourage students to use these bookmarks while they read any new text. During independent reading, students take a bookmark from the basket and color the stars that show which strategies they used. By this point, the Strategic Thinker Bookmarks will be the only visual cues students use to remind themselves to apply the strategies they have learned. Be sure to have the bookmarks available for students at all times.

978-1-4129-5824-0

Hats Off! A Reading Strategy Guide

Strategy Hats	Strategy	Student-Friendly Definition	If the Hat Fits, Wear It!
	Activating Prior Knowledge	Recalling what you already know about a topic. *I already know . . .*	A graduate has a large base of prior knowledge to draw from.
	Making Connections	Connecting the text to your own life. *It reminds me of . . .*	A cool kid propels through his or her past.
	Inferring	Using clues in the text to find deeper meaning. *The clues help me . . .*	A detective searches for clues to solve a mystery.
	Predicting	Making an educated guess. *I think . . .*	A weather forecaster tells what he or she thinks will happen in the future.
	Visualizing	Creating a mental image in your head. *I am picturing . . .*	An artist creates mental images in order to make a picture come alive.
	Questioning	Having conversations with or about the text. *I wonder . . .*	A police officer must ask questions to get to the bottom of a story.
	Monitoring and Clarifying	Thinking about your reading while fixing any mix-ups. *I can fix up my mix-ups.*	A construction worker identifies problems and fixes them.
	Searching and Selecting	Identifying necessary information in the text. *This is important because . . .*	An explorer only has time to visit the most important places.
	Summarizing	Restating the meaning of the text. *Somebody wanted . . . But . . . So then . . .*	A reporter must stick to the facts and be concise.

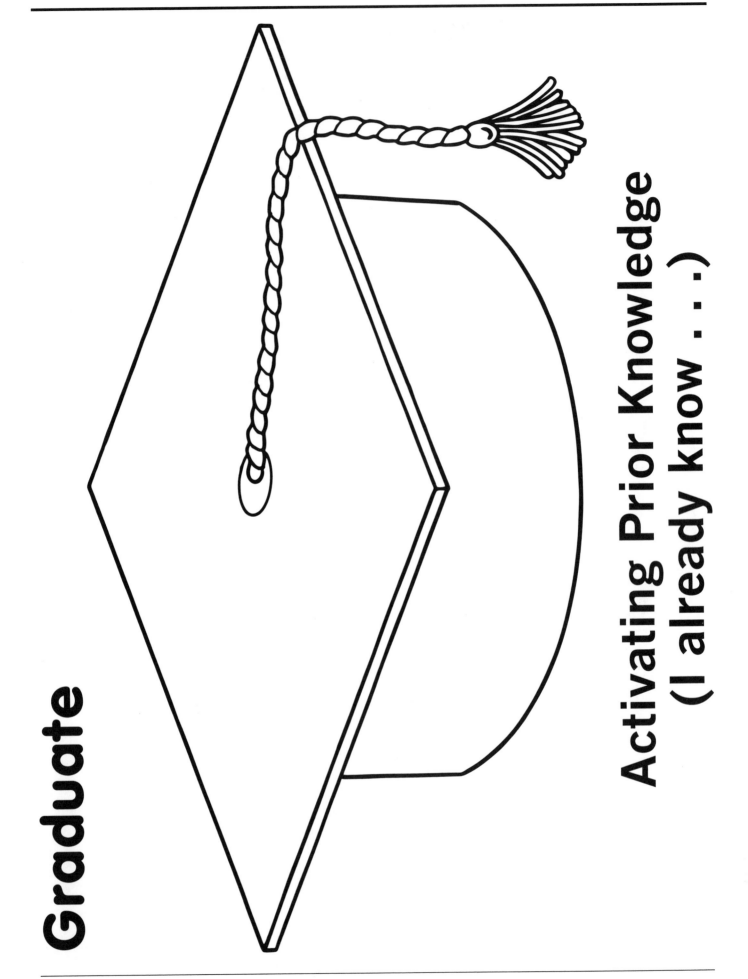

Graduate

Activating Prior Knowledge (I already know . . .)

Reproducible 978-1-4129-5824-0 • © Corwin Press

Cool Kid

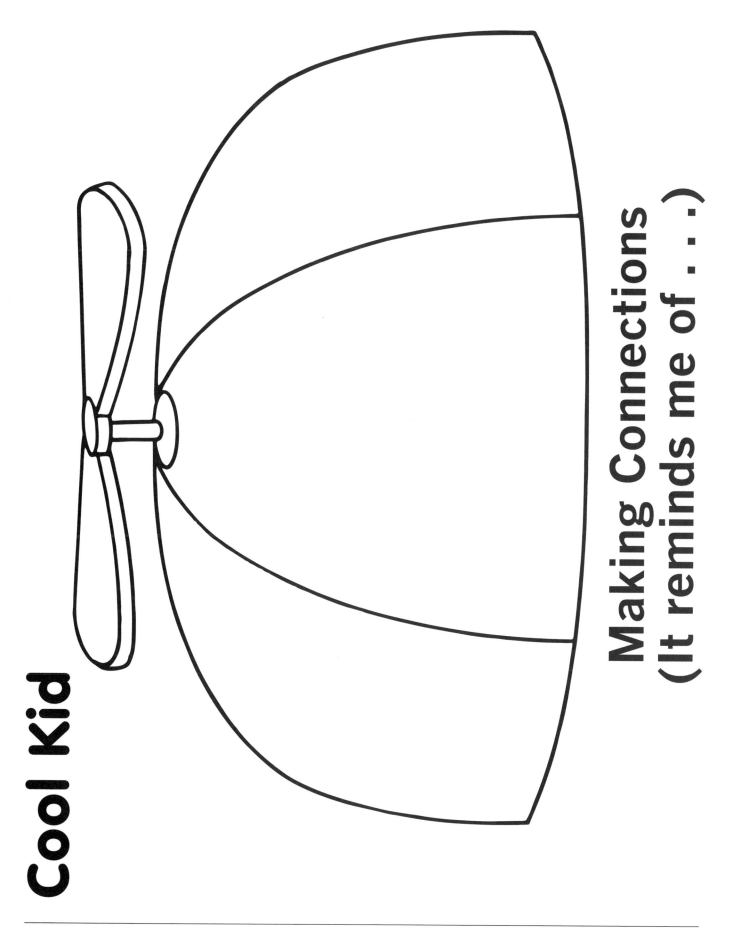

Making Connections (It reminds me of . . .)

Detective

Inferring
(The clues help me . . . .)

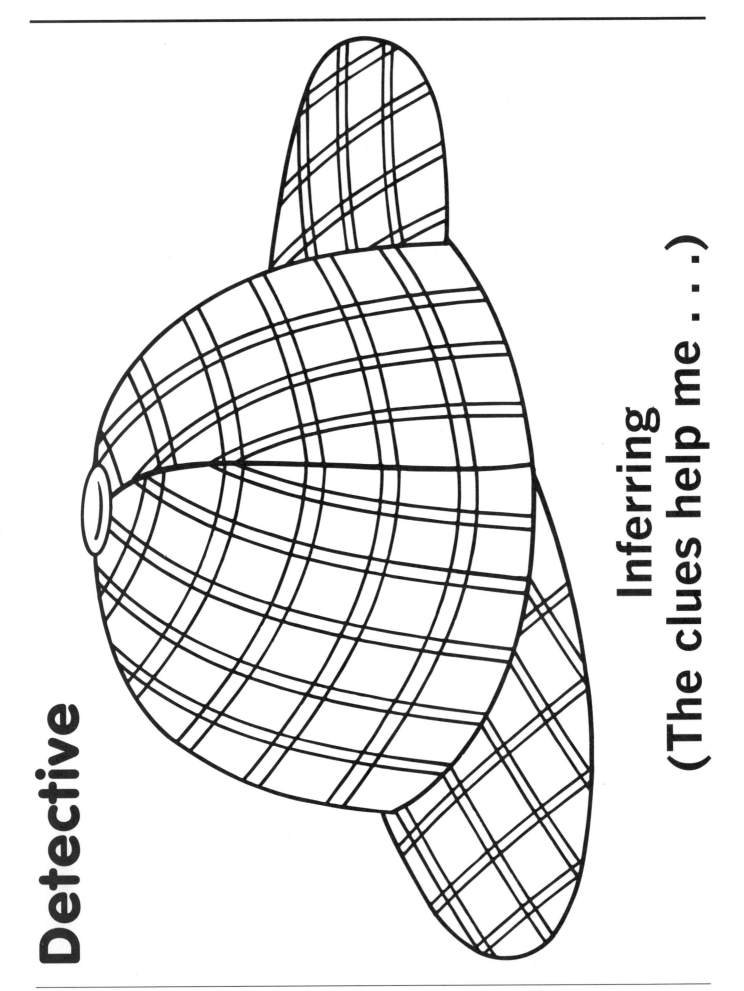

Reproducible   978-1-4129-5824-0 • © Corwin Press

Weather Forecaster

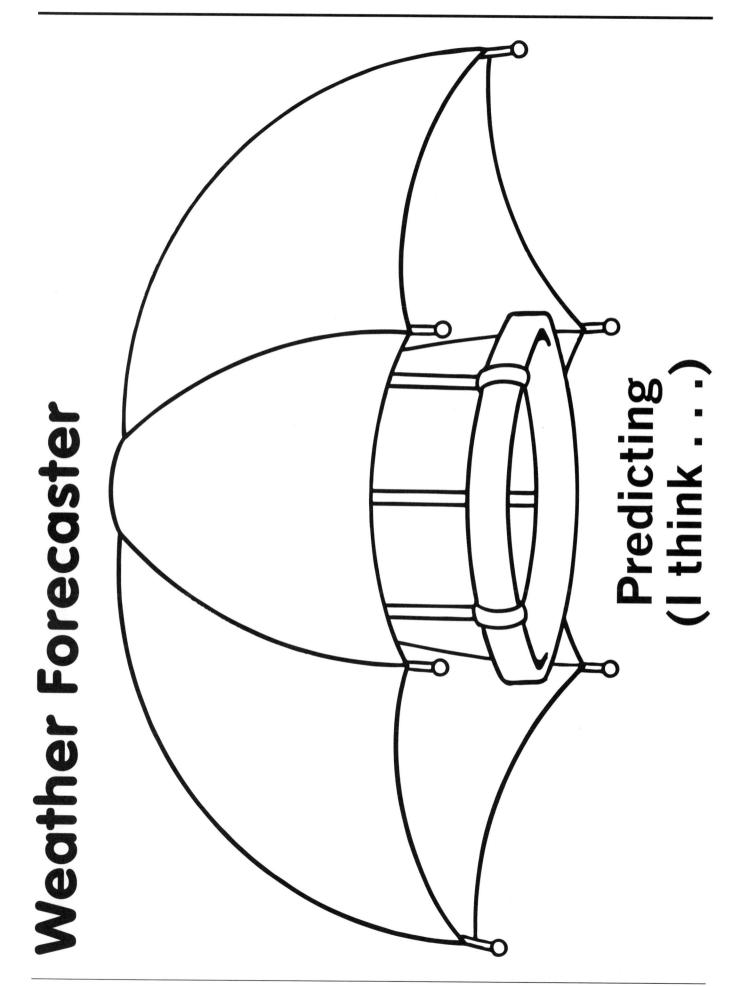

Predicting
(I think . . .)

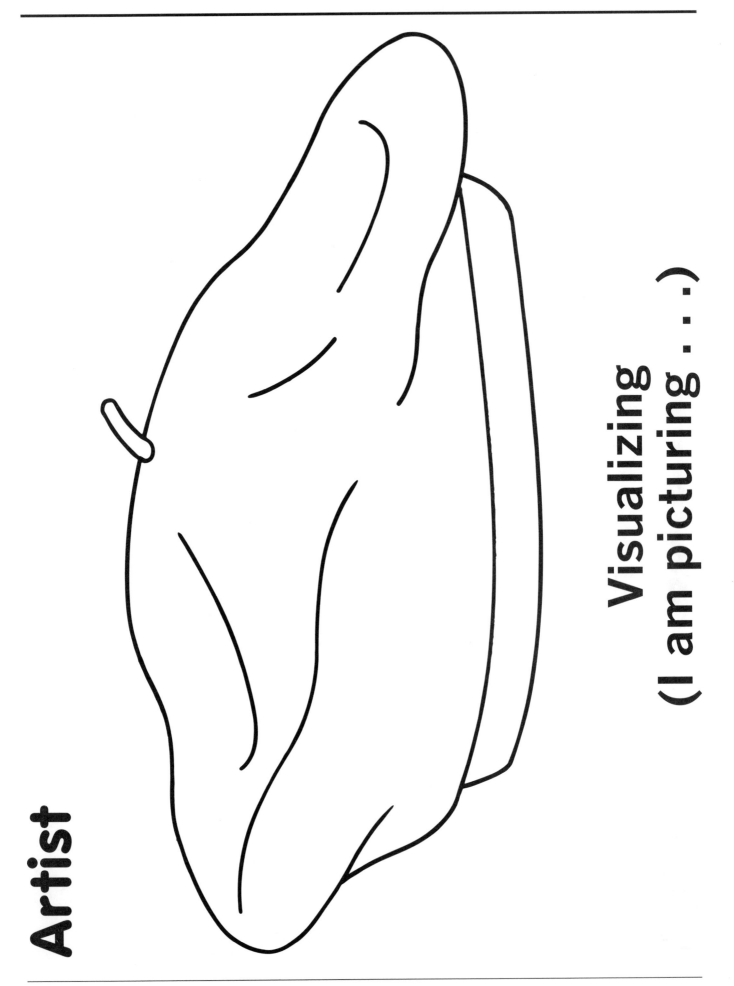

Artist

**Visualizing
(I am picturing . . .)**

Reproducible   978-1-4129-5824-0 • © *Corwin Press*

Police Officer

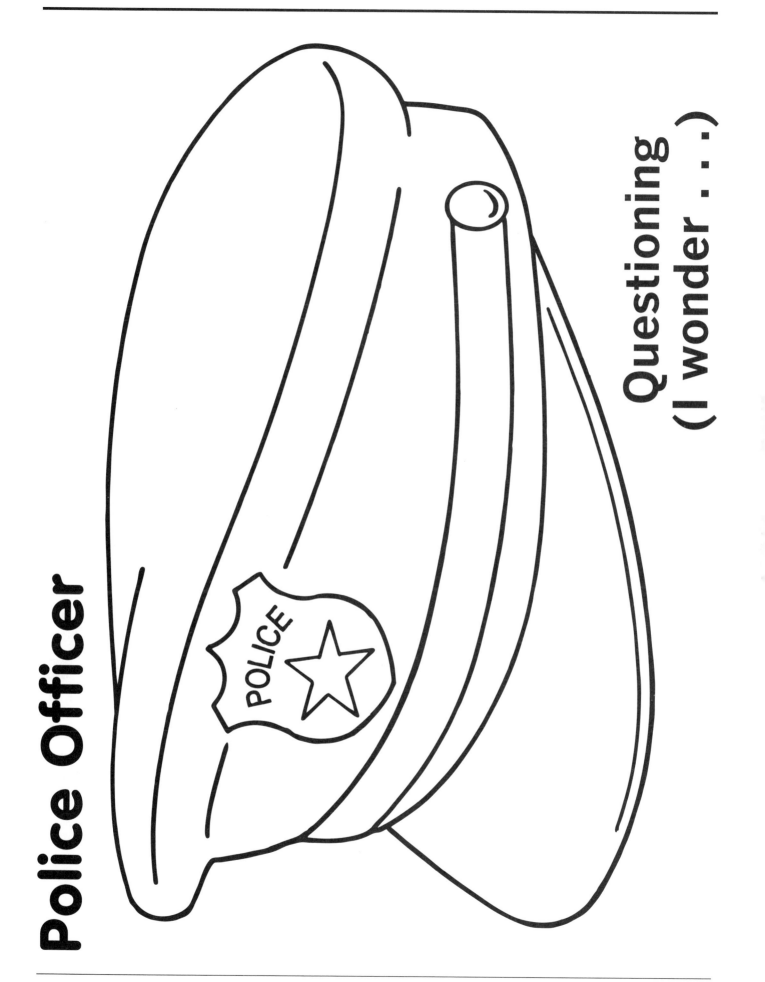

Questioning
(I wonder . . .)

Construction Worker

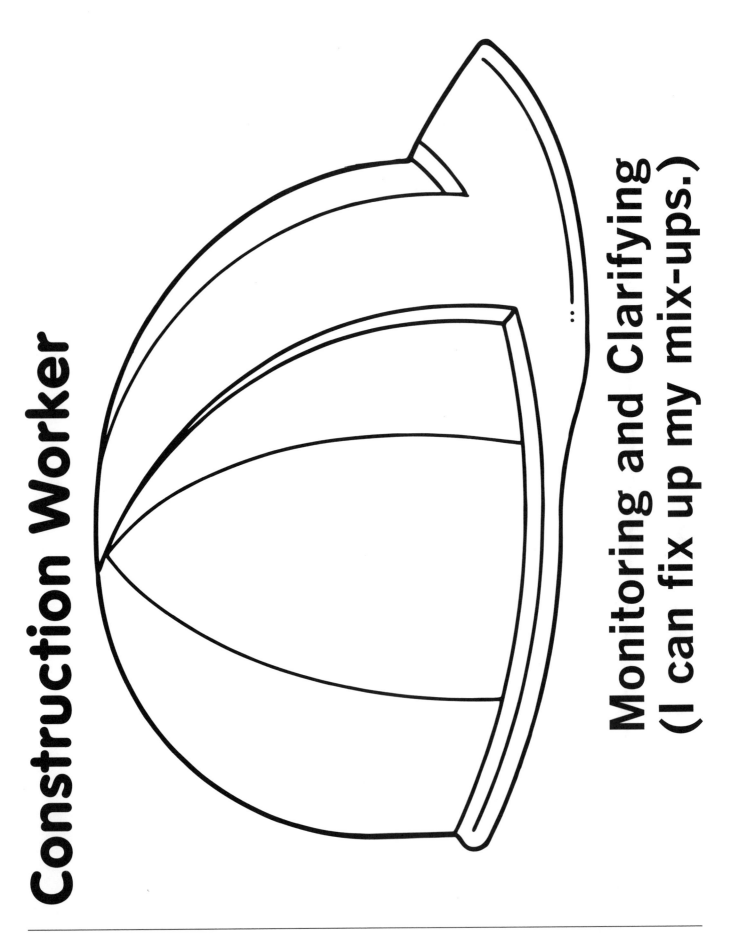

Monitoring and Clarifying
(I can fix up my mix-ups.)

Reproducible   978-1-4129-5824-0 • © Corwin Press

Explorer

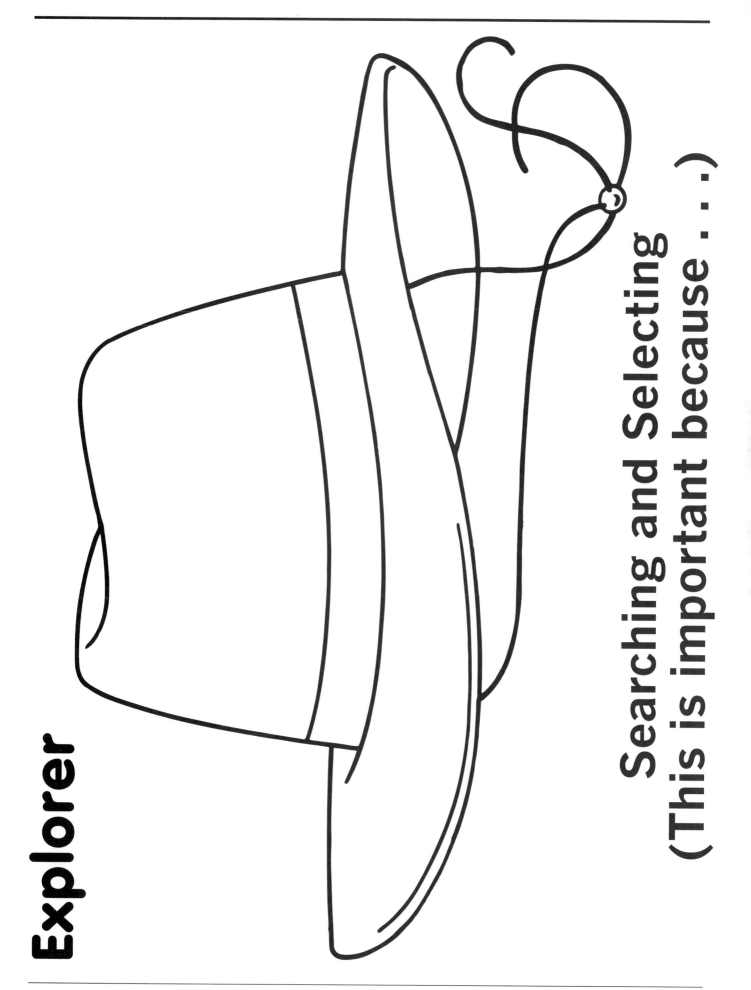

Searching and Selecting
(This is important because . . .)

Reporter

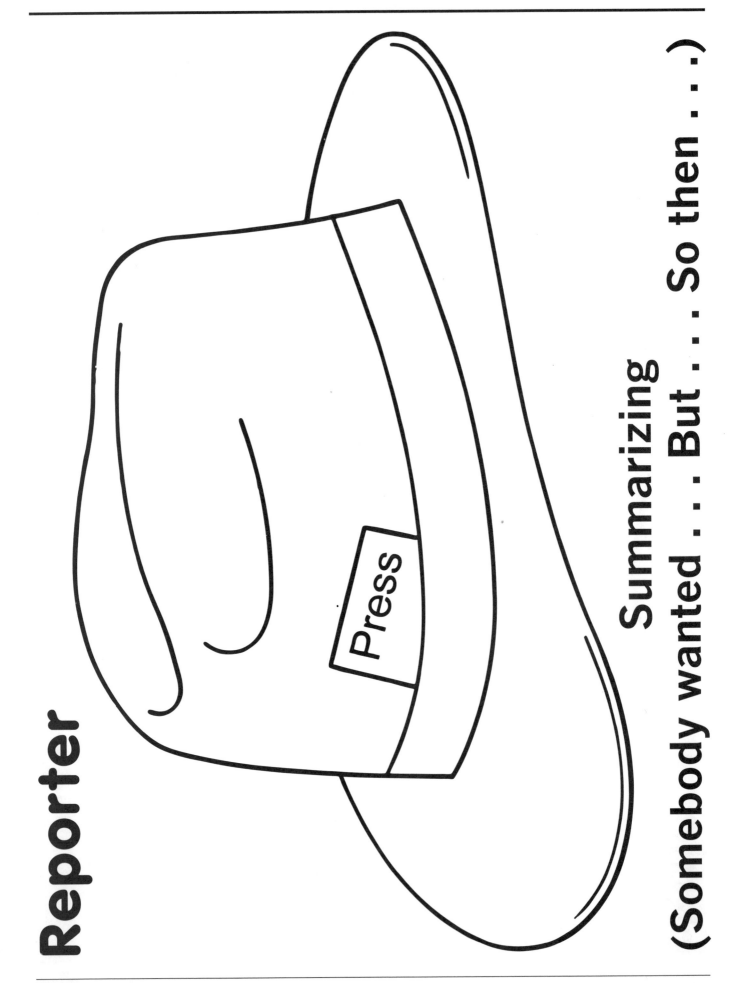

Summarizing

(Somebody wanted . . . But . . . So then . . .)

Reproducible   978-1-4129-5824-0 • © Corwin Press

Reading Strategy Cards

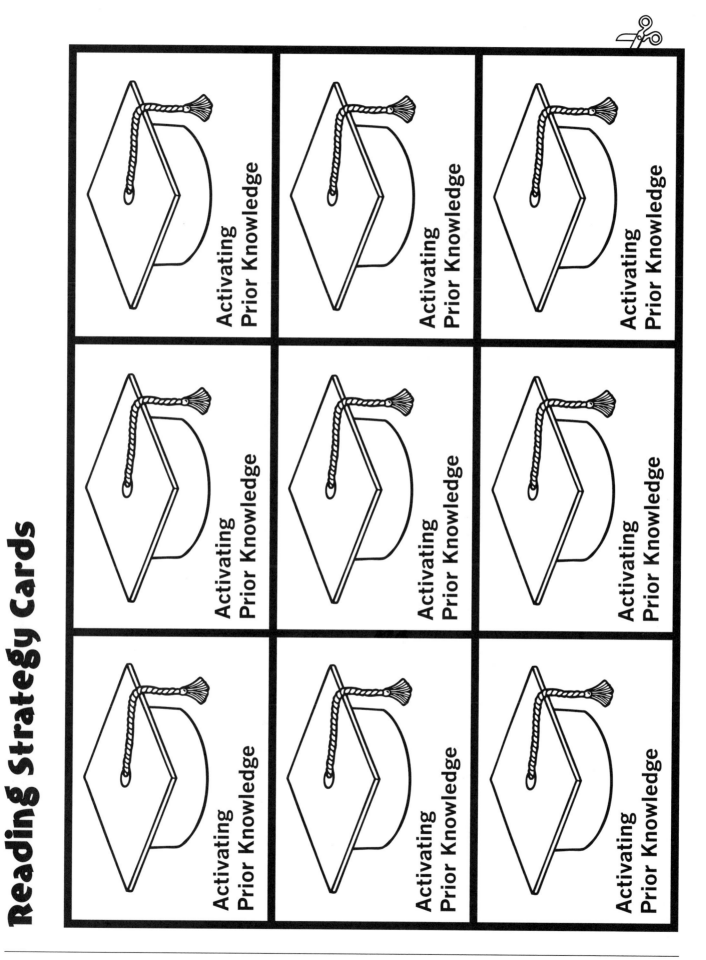

Reading Strategy Cards

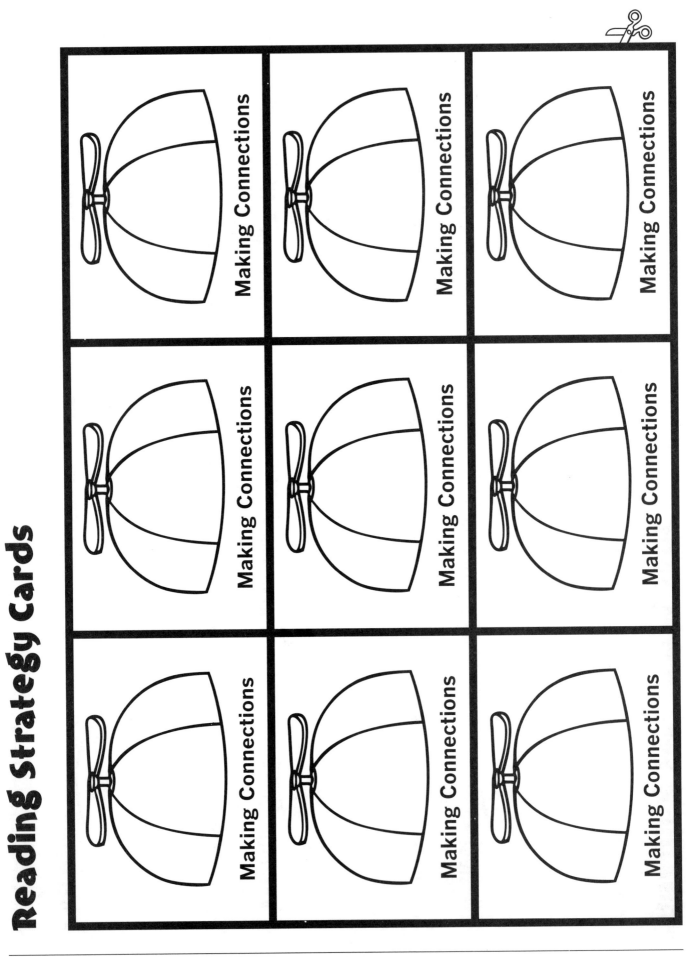

Reading Strategy Cards

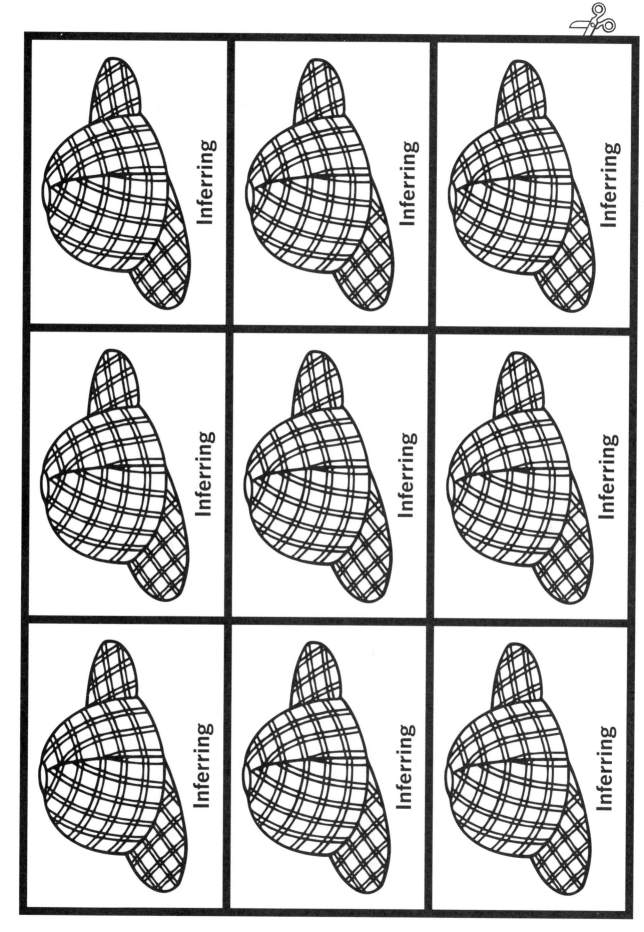

Reading Strategy Cards

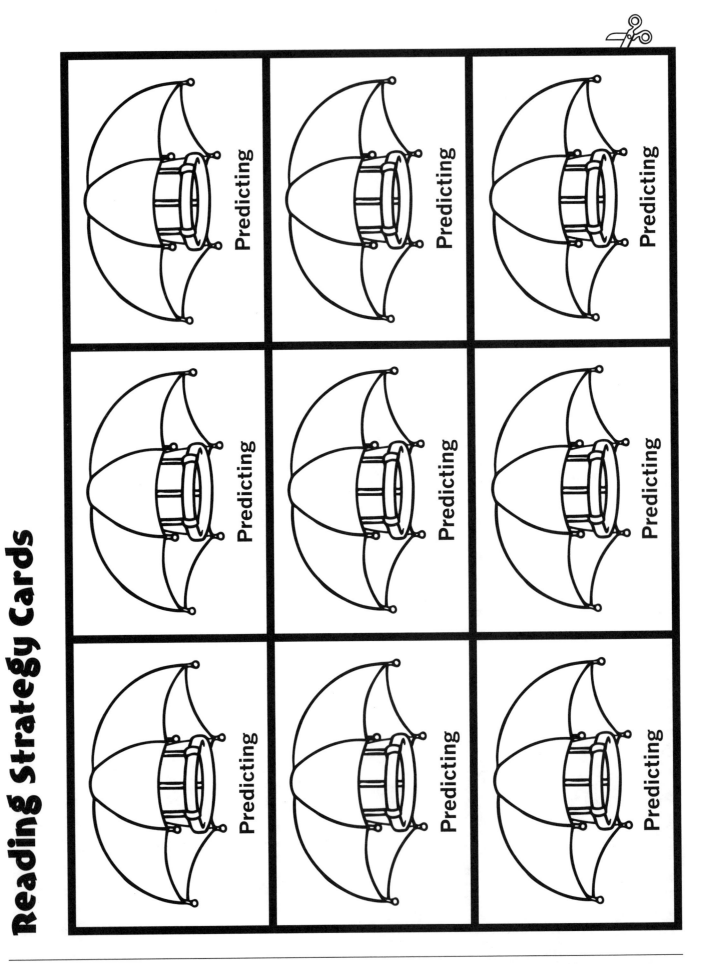

Reproducible 978-1-4129-5824-0 • © Corwin Press

Reading Strategy Cards

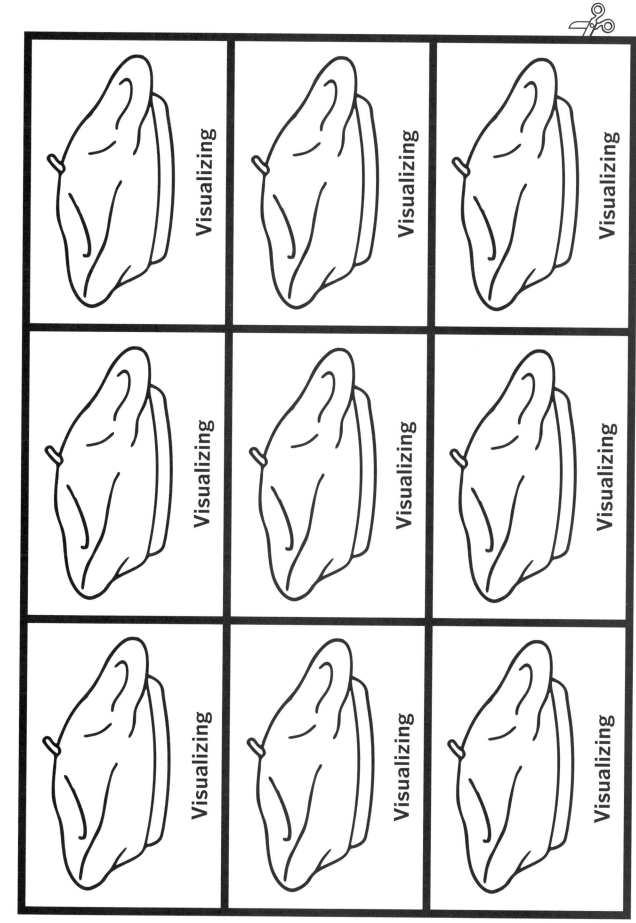

Visualizing · Visualizing · Visualizing
Visualizing · Visualizing · Visualizing
Visualizing · Visualizing · Visualizing

Reading Strategy Cards

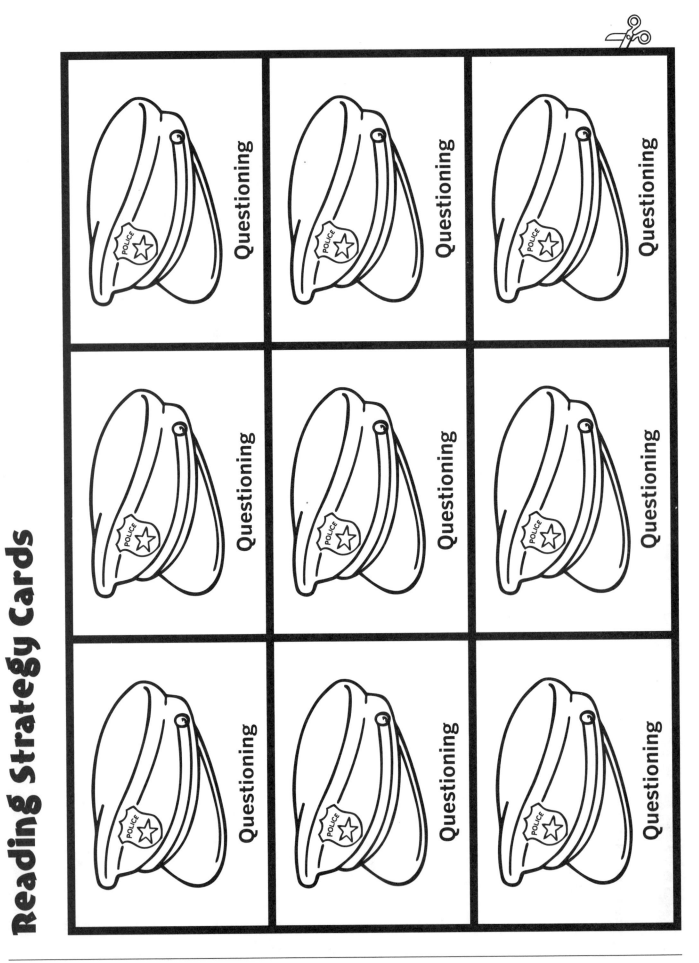

Reproducible

Reading Strategy Cards

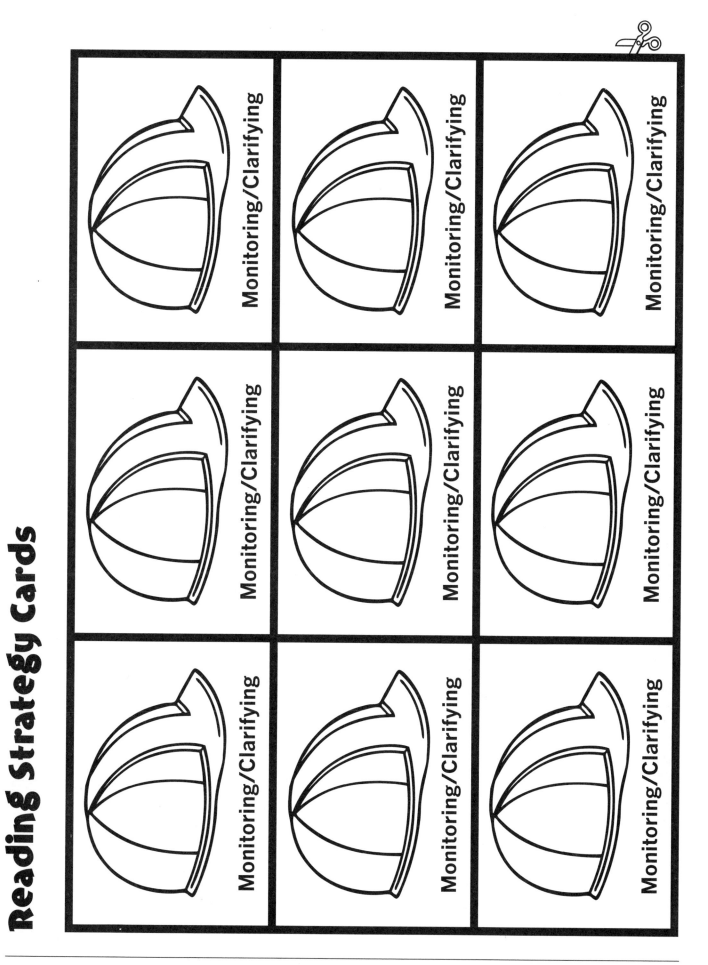

Monitoring/Clarifying

Reading Strategy Cards

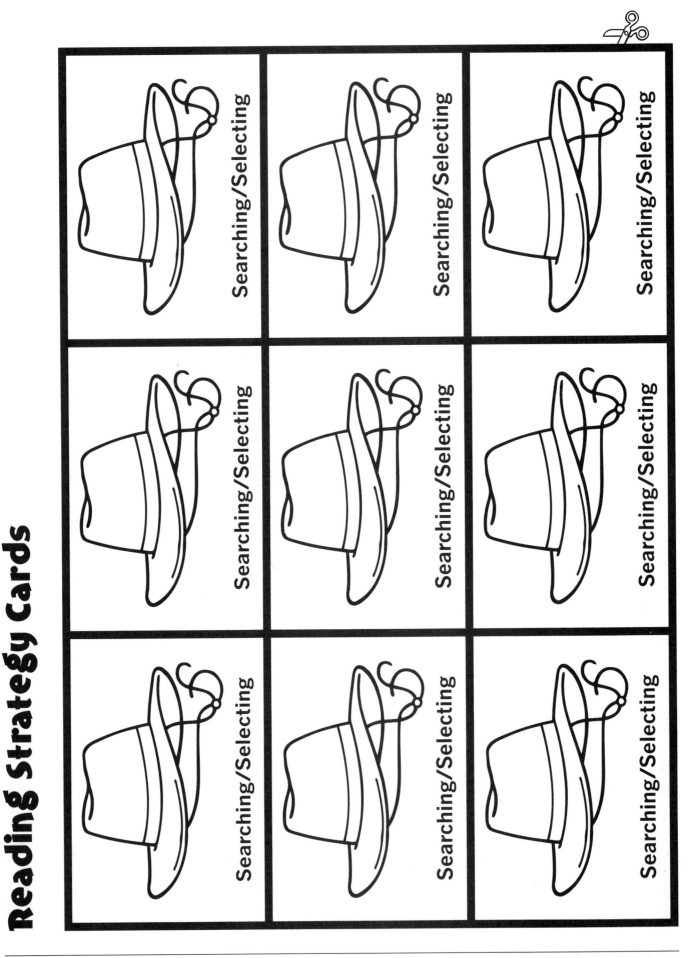

Searching/Selecting

Searching/Selecting

Searching/Selecting

Searching/Selecting

Searching/Selecting

Searching/Selecting

Searching/Selecting

Searching/Selecting

Searching/Selecting

Reproducible   978-1-4129-5824-0 • © Corwin Press

Reading Strategy Cards

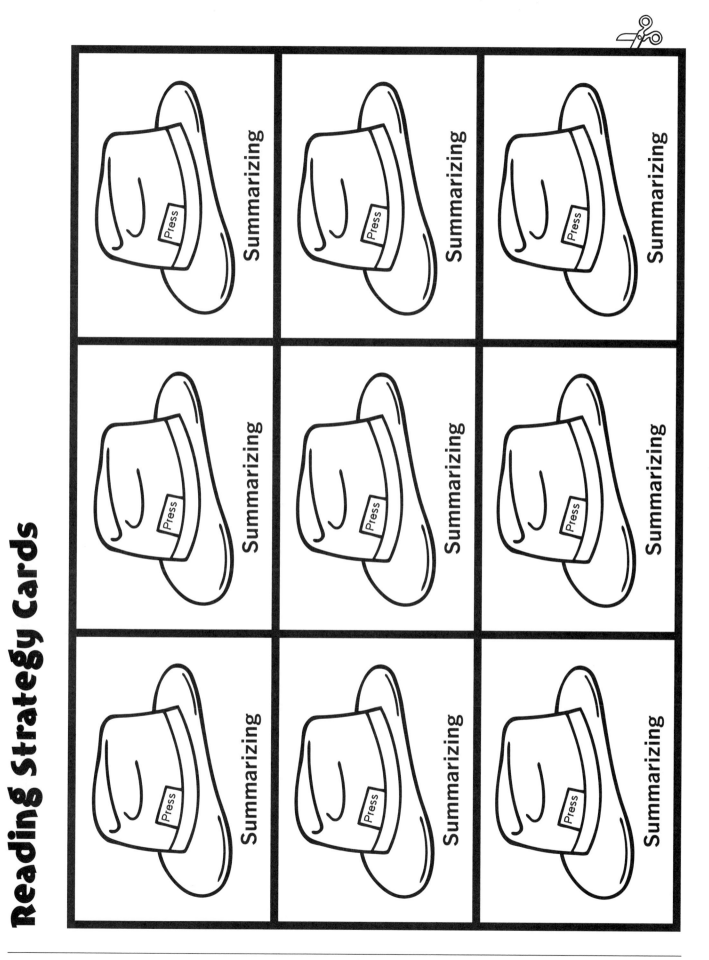

Summarizing

Summarizing

Summarizing

Summarizing

Summarizing

Summarizing

Summarizing

Summarizing

Summarizing

Reading Strategy Bookmarks

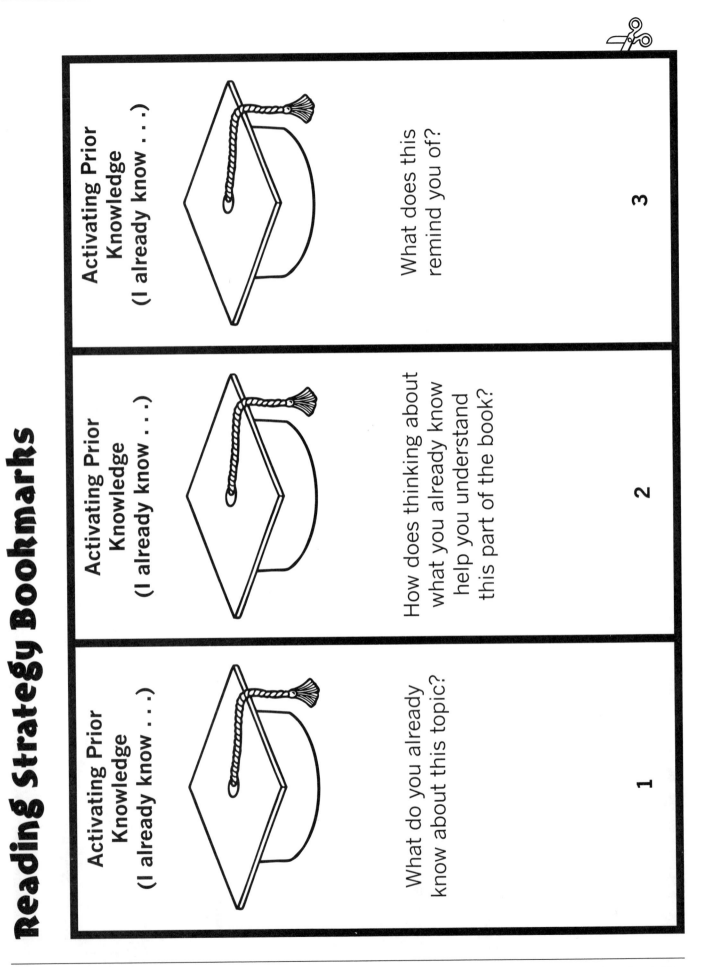

Activating Prior Knowledge (I already know . . .)

What do you already know about this topic?

1

Activating Prior Knowledge (I already know . . .)

How does thinking about what you already know help you understand this part of the book?

2

Activating Prior Knowledge (I already know . . .)

What does this remind you of?

3

Reading Strategy Bookmarks

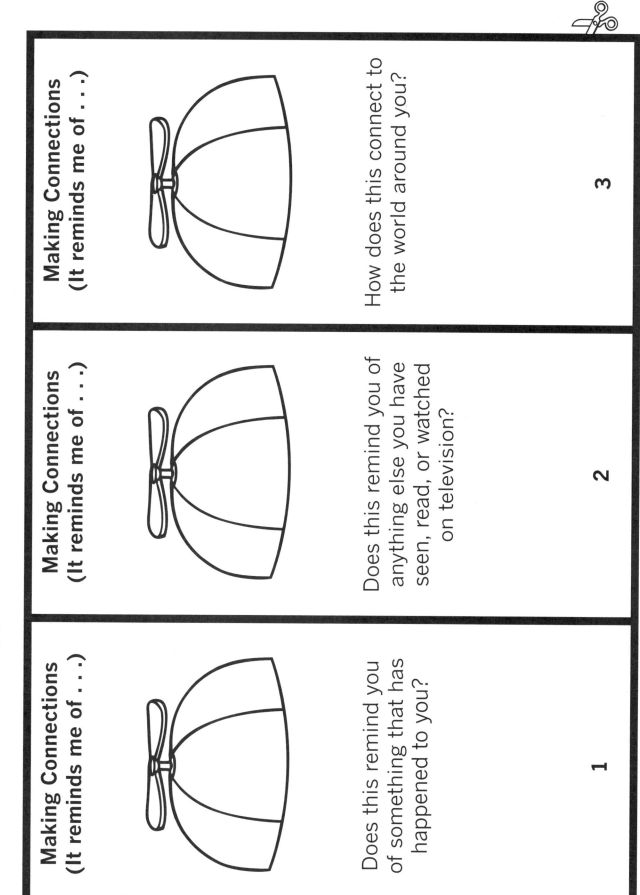

Making Connections
(It reminds me of . . .)

Does this remind you of something that has happened to you?

1

Making Connections
(It reminds me of . . .)

Does this remind you of anything else you have seen, read, or watched on television?

2

Making Connections
(It reminds me of . . .)

How does this connect to the world around you?

3

Reading Strategy Bookmarks

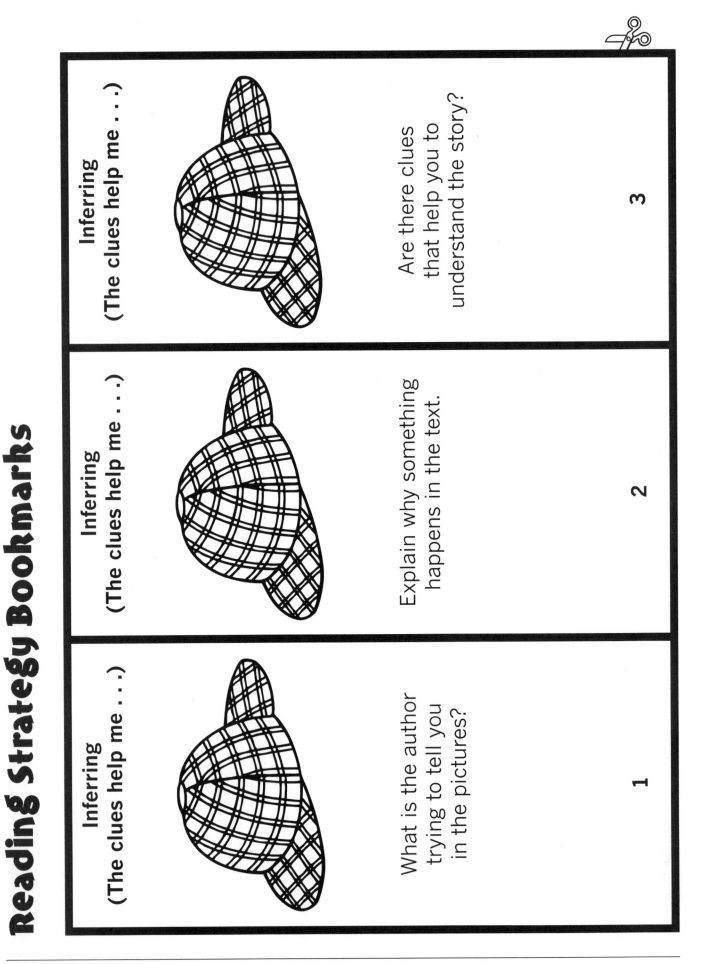

Inferring
(The clues help me . . .)

What is the author
trying to tell you
in the pictures?

1

Inferring
(The clues help me . . .)

Explain why something
happens in the text.

2

Inferring
(The clues help me . . .)

Are there clues
that help you to
understand the story?

3

Reading Strategy Bookmarks

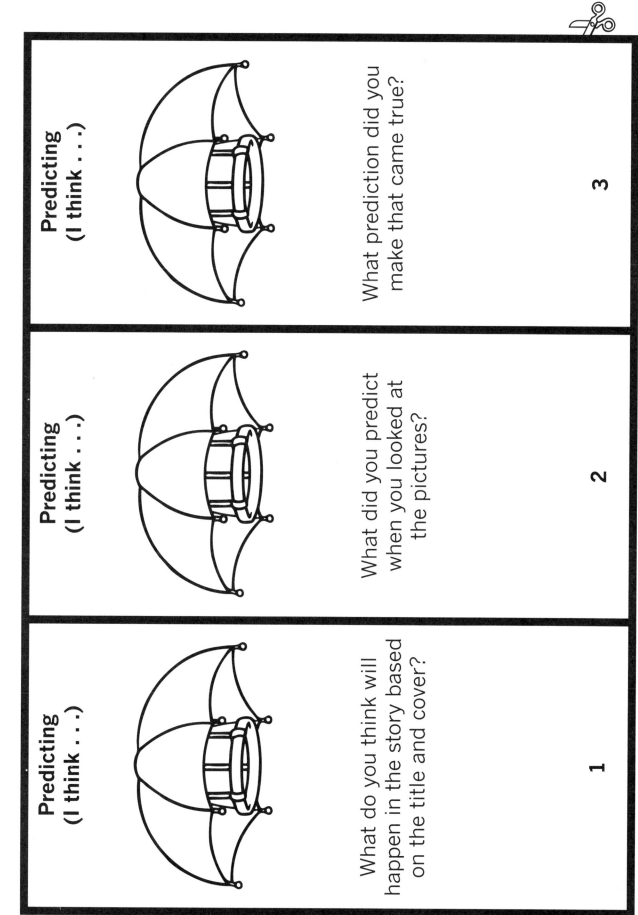

Predicting
(I think . . .)

What do you think will happen in the story based on the title and cover?

1

Predicting
(I think . . .)

What did you predict when you looked at the pictures?

2

Predicting
(I think . . .)

What prediction did you make that came true?

3

Reading Strategy Bookmarks

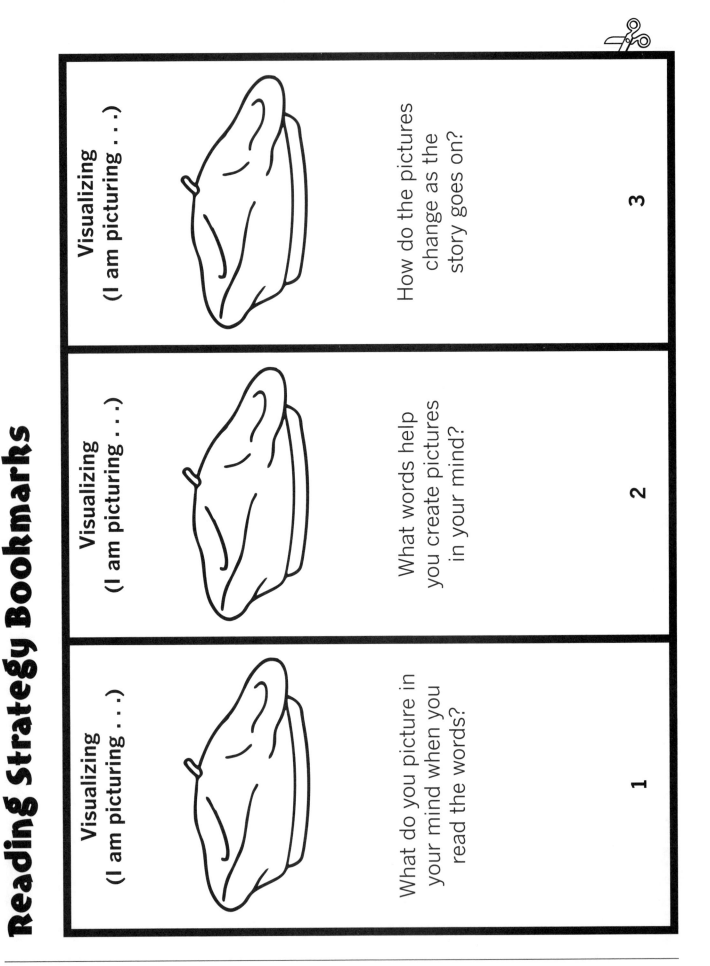

Visualizing
(I am picturing . . .)

How do the pictures change as the story goes on?

3

Visualizing
(I am picturing . . .)

What words help you create pictures in your mind?

2

Visualizing
(I am picturing . . .)

What do you picture in your mind when you read the words?

1

Reproducible

Reading Strategy Bookmarks

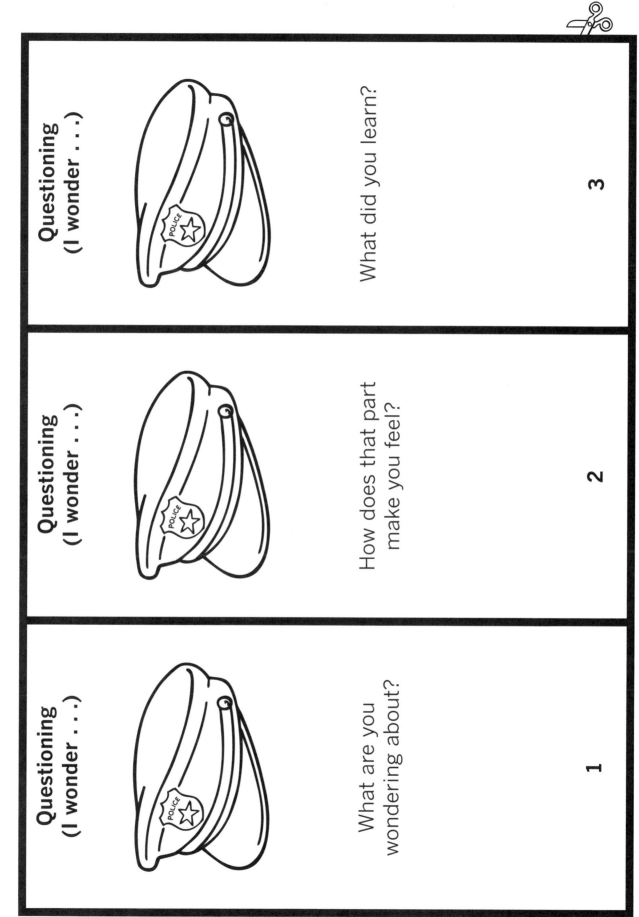

Questioning
(I wonder . . .)

What are you wondering about?

1

Questioning
(I wonder . . .)

How does that part make you feel?

2

Questioning
(I wonder . . .)

What did you learn?

3

Reading Strategy Bookmarks

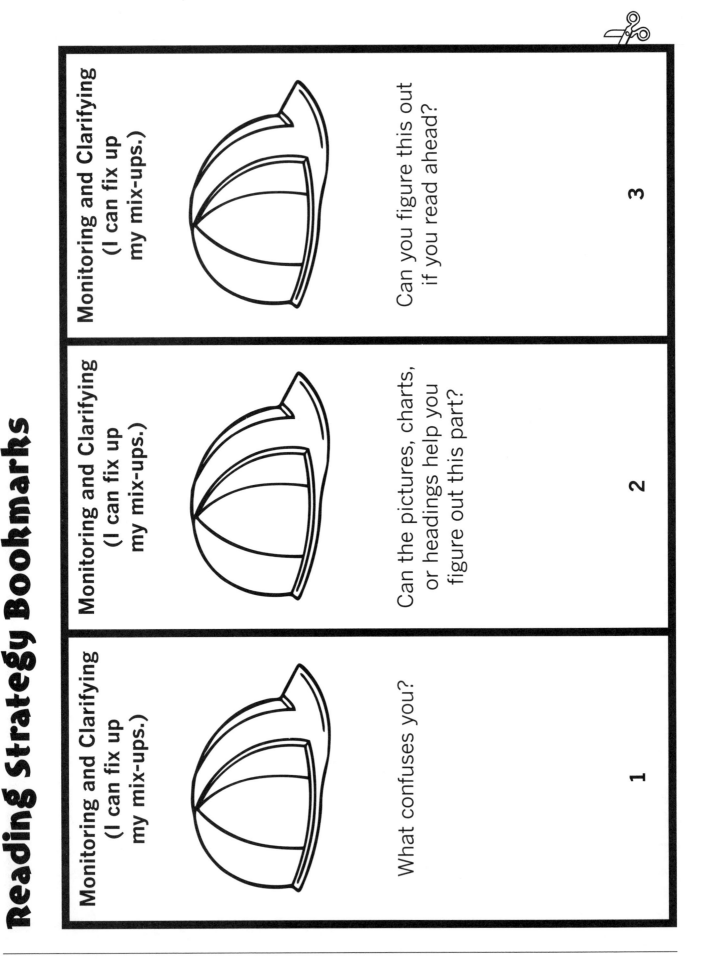

Monitoring and Clarifying
(I can fix up
my mix-ups.)

What confuses you?

1

Monitoring and Clarifying
(I can fix up
my mix-ups.)

Can the pictures, charts,
or headings help you
figure out this part?

2

Monitoring and Clarifying
(I can fix up
my mix-ups.)

Can you figure this out
if you read ahead?

3

Reading Strategy Bookmarks

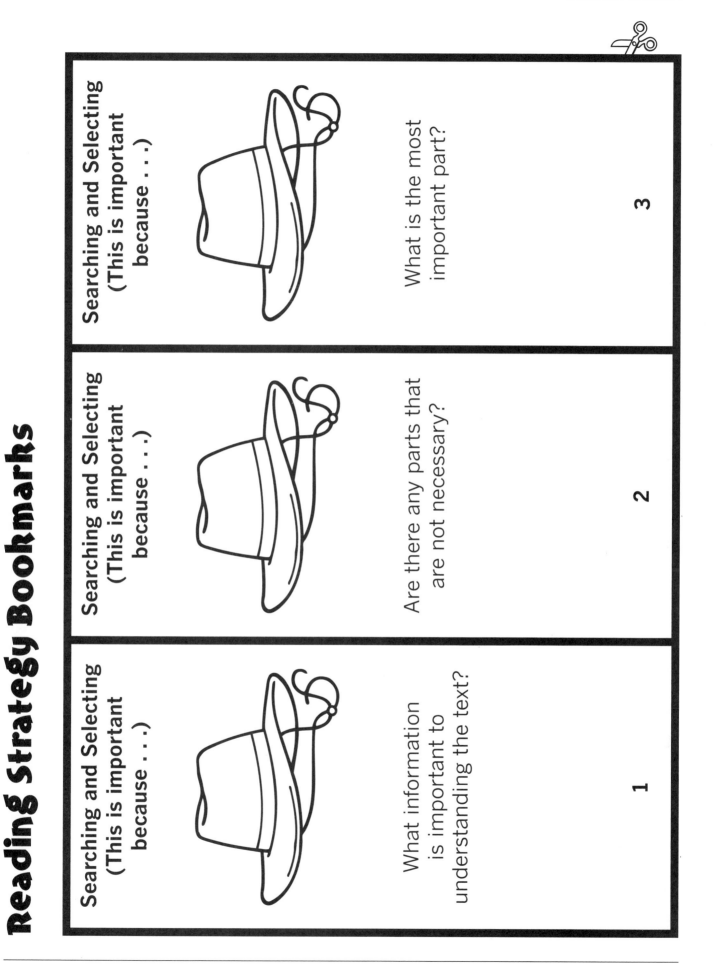

Searching and Selecting
(This is important because . . .)

What is the the most important part?

3

Searching and Selecting
(This is important because . . .)

Are there any parts that are not necessary?

2

Searching and Selecting
(This is important because . . .)

What information is important to understanding the text?

1

Reading Strategy Bookmarks

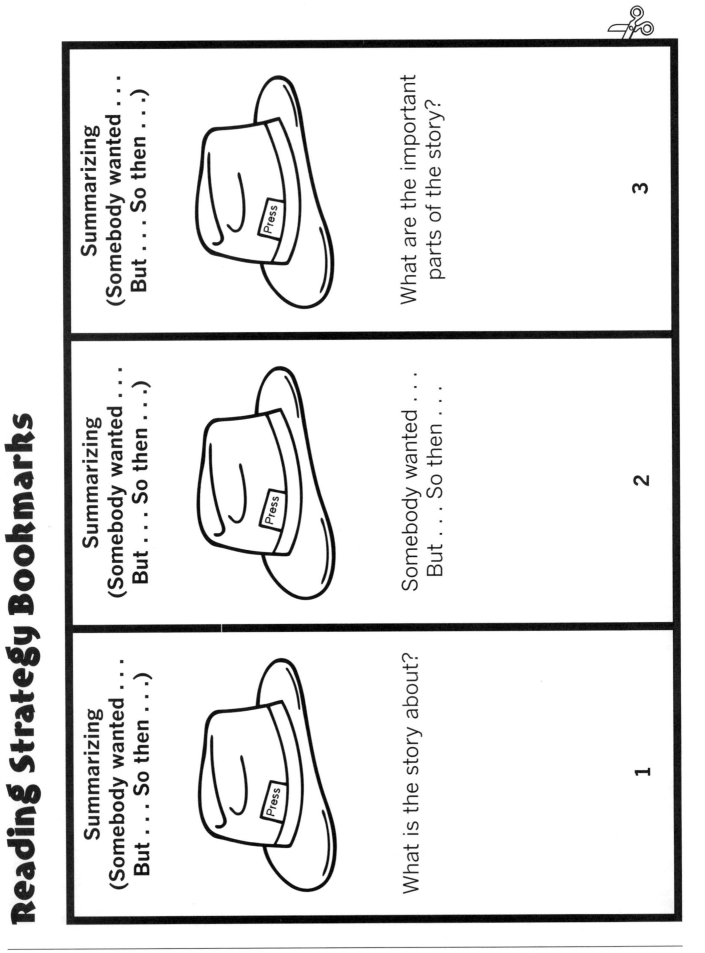

Summarizing
(Somebody wanted . . . .
But . . . So then . . . .)

Press

What are the important parts of the story?

3

Summarizing
(Somebody wanted . . . .
But . . . So then . . . .)

Press

Somebody wanted . . . .
But . . . So then . . . .

2

Summarizing
(Somebody wanted . . . .
But . . . So then . . . .)

Press

What is the story about?

1

Strategic Thinker Bookmarks

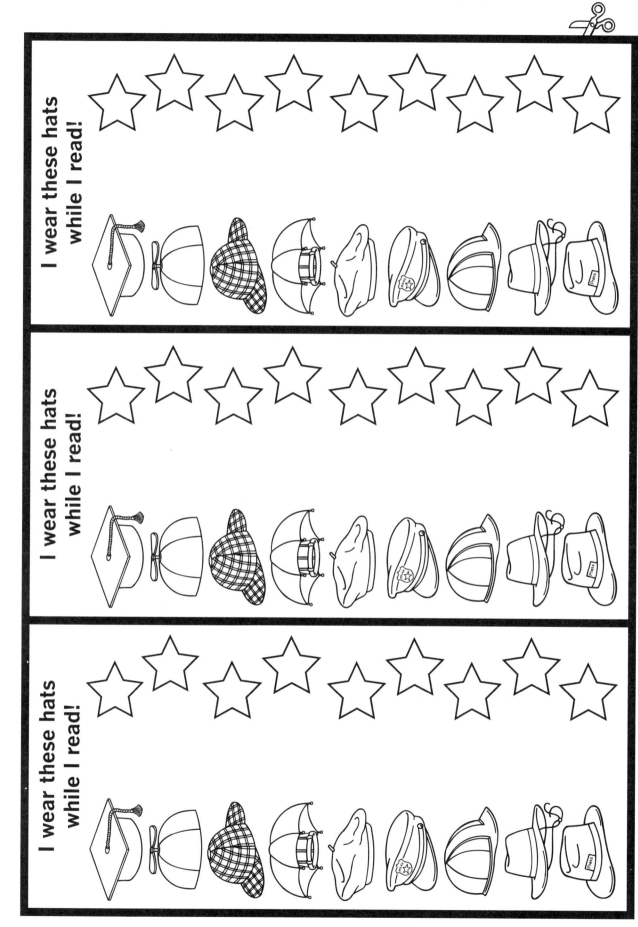

I wear these hats while I read!

I wear these hats while I read!

I wear these hats while I read!

CHAPTER 2

A Hat Full of Tricks

Activating Prior Knowledge

Building your students' background knowledge is an important first step in preparing them to read. Activating their prior knowledge will not only help increase students' understanding of the story or text, but it will also stimulate their interest and motivation. As students share their personal schema, they begin to take ownership of the text, increase their curiosity, and become engrossed in what they read. Discussing ideas and concepts before reading provides a foundation on which new ideas and information can build.

Activation Station

Prior to introducing a new concept or story to students, tell them that you would like their help. You might explain that you are planning for the upcoming lesson, and it happens to be about a topic that is new to you. Tell them that you would like their help in order to be better prepared to teach this lesson. Create a special area in the classroom called the Activation Station. It could be a table or desk with a bulletin board behind it. Make the station look appealing and post the name of the topic or book there.

Ask students to help you by thinking about the topic and activating their prior knowledge. Explain that because of our prior knowledge, we can all contribute something different to our learning. When we add up what we know as a group, we build our prior knowledge.

Give students a copy of the **Activation Station Note Cards reproducible (page 40)**. Explain that their homework will be to fill out one of the cards with something they already know about the topic. On the other card, they will write about something they would like to learn about the topic. Students may also bring in photos, books, poems, or anything else related to the topic. Place the items in the Activation Station, along with the note cards, in order to help activate the prior knowledge of other students in the class. Each day, take a few minutes to introduce any new items placed in the Activation Station and read the note cards.

As you introduce each new concept or story, allow students an opportunity to share their knowledge and understanding. In this way, you will actively engage them in the process of learning new concepts and information. The Activation Station will become a new and exciting place to share and activate prior knowledge!

Name ____________________ Date ____________________

Activation Station Note Cards

Directions: Think about ________________. On the first card, write one interesting **fact** you know about the topic. On the second card, write a **question** or something you want to learn about the topic. Please return the cards tomorrow so we can put them in our Activation Station. Thank you!

I already know . . .

____

____

____

____

I would like to know . . .

____

____

____

____

978-1-4129-5824-0 •

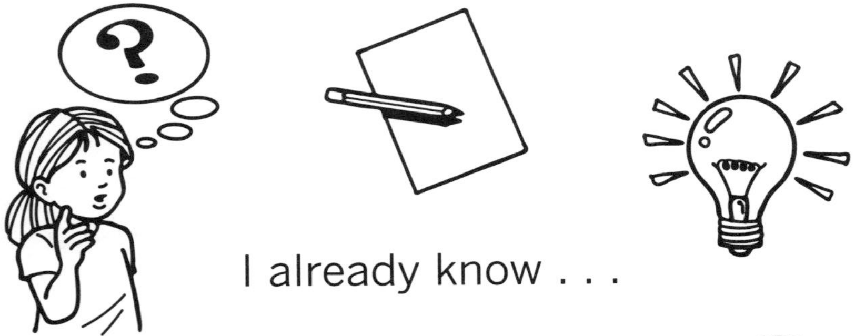

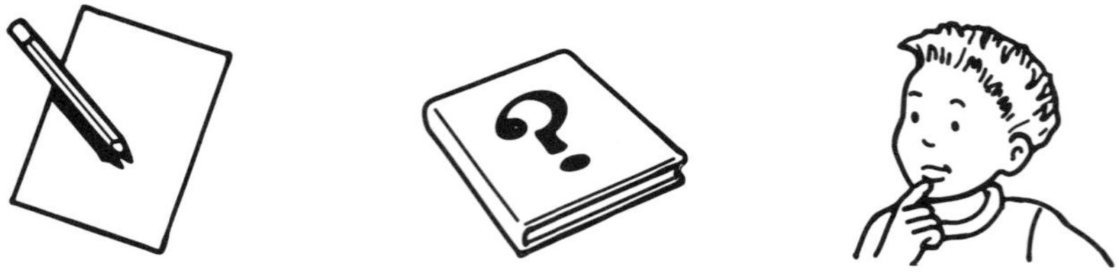

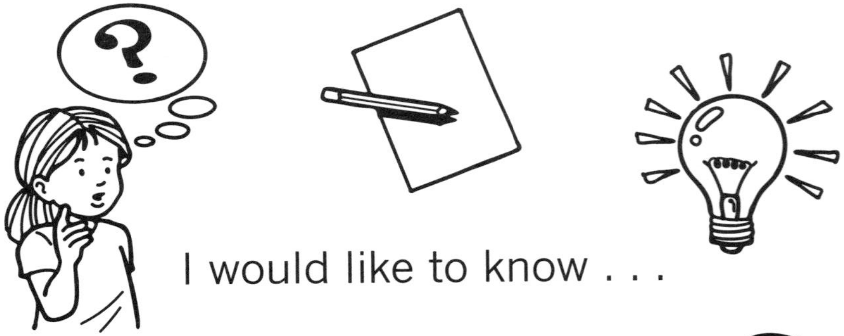

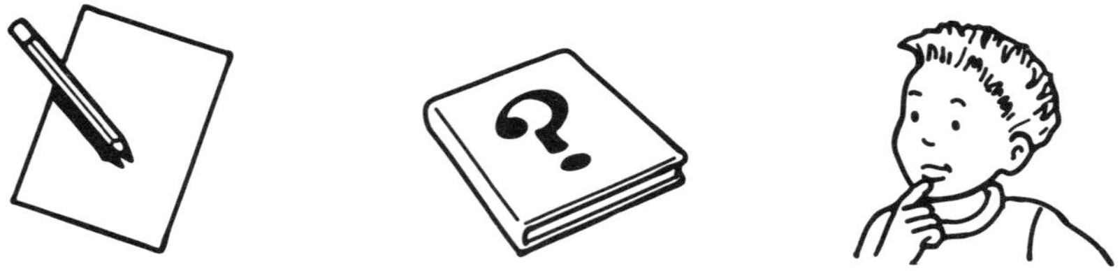

Sticky Business

What better way to get your students actively engaged in a lesson than to let them share their prior knowledge with friends? When introducing a new literature theme or concept, ask for a volunteer from the class to become the "prior knowledge expert."

Have the volunteer stand next to you in front of the class. Write the topic or theme on a sentence strip, attach a piece of string to it, and hang it around the student's neck. Explain to the other students that their job is to help "fill" the class expert with prior knowledge. Have the expert call on volunteers to share something they already know about the topic. Quickly jot the information on sticky notes and attach them to the expert's sign. Make chains of notes by attaching them to other notes. Your students will be able to clearly see the sum total of their knowledge grow.

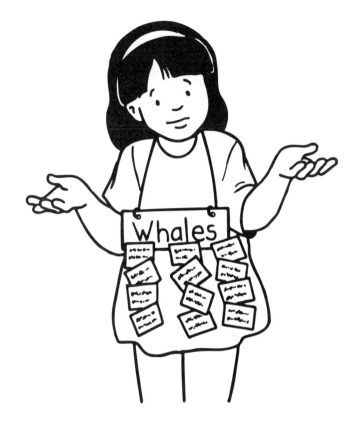

Making Connections

Encouraging students to make connections to themselves, to other texts, and to the world during reading instruction is like having a show-and-tell session. It is a great strategy because children enjoy sharing stories and experiences that are close to their hearts. It gives them the opportunity to become involved in the process of personal engagement while improving their comprehension and understanding. As skilled readers move through a text, they constantly compare and contrast their knowledge and experience with that text. Accomplished readers often make connections to their lives, to other texts they have read, and to the world they are coming to know.

Goldilocks's Collection of Connections

The following Reader's Theater selection, **Goldilocks's Connections (pages 42–44)** is a fun and exciting way to introduce your class to the concept of making connections. Following their performance of "Goldilocks's Connections," lead students in a discussion of the various ways the characters used the strategy of making connections.

Goldilocks's Connections

Narrator 1: One day, a little girl named Goldilocks was walking through the woods. She came upon a house and wondered who lived inside.

Narrator 2: Goldilocks decided to take a peek through the window.

Goldilocks: It looks like no one is home.

Narrator 3: Goldilocks saw that there was a whole bookshelf filled with books.

Narrator 1: She loved to read books and wanted very badly to go inside to see if there were any that she would enjoy. As she stepped inside, Goldilocks noticed something hanging on the wall.

Goldilocks: Wow! There is a picture of a bear family reading together. This house must belong to a family of bears!

Narrator 2: Goldilocks then noticed that there was some porridge on the table. Feeling hungry, she first tried Papa Bear's porridge.

Goldilocks: That porridge is too hot!

Narrator 3: Mama Bear's porridge was too cold. Then Goldilocks tried Baby Bear's porridge.

Goldilocks: Yum! This is just right! It reminds me of the oatmeal that I eat for breakfast.

Narrator 1: Goldilocks went into the reading room to find a good book to read.

Goldilocks's Connections (cont.)

Narrator 2: She found the perfect book and sat down in each chair—Papa Bear's, Mama Bear's, and Baby Bear's.

Goldilocks: This chair is too hard! And this chair is too soft. Now, this chair reminds me of my comfy chair at home. It is just right.

Narrator 3: Goldilocks began reading the book, *Frog and Toad Together.* Just then, she heard the bears walking in the door.

Goldilocks: Oh no! They're home!

Narrator 1: As the bears walked into the room to enjoy a family read-aloud, they noticed Goldilocks sitting in Baby Bear's chair.

Baby Bear: What are you doing in my chair?

Goldilocks: I'm very sorry. I just love reading books, so I decided to stay and enjoy this book.

Mama Bear: Would you like to join us for a read-aloud?

Goldilocks: Sure, that would be great! I just started taking a picture walk through *Frog and Toad Together.*

Baby Bear: I love that story. It reminds me of being together with my family.

Papa Bear: That's a great connection, Baby Bear. Good readers always make connections when they read.

Goldilocks's Connections (cont.)

Goldilocks: Before you came home I was trying to figure out the word *together*. I remembered that my friend and I play outside *together*. That connection helped me figure out the word.

Narrator 2: Goldilocks and the three bears started to read the first story, "Tomorrow." Mama Bear thought of a connection to the story.

Mama Bear: The part of the story that says the house is a mess reminded me of yesterday. Our house was very messy, and we had a lot of chores to do.

Papa Bear: This story reminds me of something, too. It reminds me of another Frog and Toad story called "The List." Frog and Toad had so many things to do that they made a list.

Baby Bear: You're right, Dad. Here's another connection. Yesterday we made a list of chores to do around the house. Then we all worked together to get the chores done faster. It is so much fun making connections!

Mama Bear: Because both of these stories are about cleaning up, they make me think of how everyone needs to work together to keep our forest clean. If we didn't, our world would be full of garbage.

Goldilocks: I never used to make connections while reading, but I have learned so much from you. I now understand what this book is about. We have made so many connections today. May I come over and read with you again tomorrow?

Papa Bear: That would be great!

Quirky Connections

This activity provides strategies to help students make connections that may be less obvious. If students practice making more difficult connections, it will become easier for them to apply this strategy when reading independently.

To begin the activity, read the first "quirky" connection to the class: *A baby is like a clock.* Have students brainstorm some ways in which the two subjects could be connected. Tell them there are no right or wrong answers, but they are expected to explain their reasoning. (An answer that doesn't seem to make sense at first might make sense after they hear the reasons.) Below are just a few examples of "quirky" connections that can be adapted to any grade level.

- *A baby is like a clock.* (Both move slowly, have hands, and a face.)

- *Homework is like hair.* (Both can be messy. Some people have more than others. People can help you fix them.)

- *Snakes are like kites.* (Both can slither—snakes on the ground, kites in the air. They have long tails. They can make sudden, unexpected movements.)

- *Anger is like a road.* (Both could lead you in the wrong direction. They could be full of danger.)

- *Pencils are like grass.* (Both leave stains on your pants. Kids try to chew them. Both grow, since pencils are made from trees.)

- *A stool is like a spider.* (Both have legs. You can step on them. You are bigger than they are. They can be found in a house.)

- *Eyeglasses are like a rock.* (Both are hard. They will hurt your feet if you step on them barefoot. They come in many colors.)

- *A bunny is like a cloud.* (Both are soft, can be white, are fluffy, and move. They remind us of spring.)

- *My dad is like a tree.* (Both are tall. They have big arms. You can lean on them.)

- *A shoe is like an airplane.* (Both help you get from one place to another. People need them. They come in different sizes.)

Inferring

Inferring is an important comprehension skill, and even very young students can learn to use inferential thinking in order to derive deeper meaning from text. When teaching inferential thinking, explain to students that they make inferences every day in their own lives. Possibly without even being aware of it, they are acting like detectives, gathering clues all day long. They might be looking at a picture, listening to one side of a phone conversation, or reading people's facial expressions. As they do so, they are drawing conclusions in order to gain meaning and understanding from the situation.

A Picture Is Worth a Thousand Words

Photocopy one of the "detective scene" reproducibles for this activity, **The Zoo**, **Going Camping**, or **Elementary Classroom (pages 48–50)**. Depending on the grade level you are teaching, this lesson can be done verbally as a group or by having individual students write their answers to the questions on the answer sheet reproducible, **Pictures Tell a Story (page 51)**.

Explain to students that they will need to use their best detective skills in order to identify the clues, draw conclusions, and answer the list of questions below the picture. Introduce the scene to students by telling them that it is a picture in need of a story. Like most detectives, they are given only a little bit of information. They need to come up with the rest of the story by identifying the clues. When making inferences, they must be able to back up their conclusions with "evidence" from the picture.

If you are doing the activity with a group, read each question aloud to students. Have them study the scene and raise their hands if they think they can answer the question. Be sure to have students explain the thinking process they used to unravel the clues needed to answer each question. Once students fully understand how to do this activity, give them a copy of a different "detective scene" reproducible to complete on their own, using the answer sheet provided. Remind them that they will need to explain which clues from the picture helped them to arrive at their answers.

Teacher Tip: Create other detective scenes from real photographs, comic strips, or magazine pictures. Simply create a list of your own inferential questions and photocopy them at the bottom of the picture.

As Inquisitive as a Detective

Watch your students become as inquisitive as detectives as they play this word game using the Phrase Puzzles below. This game is designed to develop their ability to use inferential thinking.

Prepare for the game by photocopying and cutting apart the similes and placing them inside a "detective hat." Tell students to sit in a circle on the carpet.

Introduce the word game. In this game, students must make inferences in order to complete the phrase puzzles. Explain that you will read the first phrase, and they should think of a word that completes the puzzle. You will go around the circle and give each student a chance to call out his or her word. However, students cannot repeat any of their classmates' answers. When students are unable to think of new words, draw a new simile from the detective hat and begin a new round. Combining clues from the phrase puzzles with students' background knowledge develops students' ability to make inferences.

Phrase Puzzles

As tall as _____.	As pretty as _____.	As silly as _____.	As smart as _____.	As dirty as _____.
As low as _____.	As friendly as _____.	As sharp as _____.	As fuzzy as _____.	As scratchy as _____.
As crazy as _____.	As yummy as _____.	As thin as _____.	As cool as _____.	As dark as _____.
As cute as _____.	As hungry as _____.	As straight as _____.	As funny as _____.	As soft as _____.
As cold as _____.	As sweet as _____.	As angry as _____.	As dry as _____.	As hot as _____.

The Zoo

1. Which animal is the zookeeper going to feed?
2. Why is the girl crying?
3. What animal is not in its pen?
4. What time of day is it?
5. Which animals can the children pet?
6. Did the children near the lion's pen come with their parents?
7. How did the peacock get out of its pen?
8. Are the children having a good time at the zoo?
9. Does the zoo have a snack bar?
10. Who would write with his left hand?

Going Camping

1. What time of day is it?
2. Who do you think is planning on going swimming today?
3. Why is there a bag up in the tree?
4. How many people are in this family?
5. Who is in the tent sleeping?
6. Why is Mom hanging the clothes?
7. Why is the little girl sad?
8. What do you think the family is going to do today?
9. What jobs do Mom and Dad have?
10. Where is the family from?

Elementary Classroom

1. How many students are absent?
2. Where do you think the missing student is?
3. Which student is left-handed?
4. What subject will the students be learning next?
5. Why do you think the little girl is unhappy?
6. Will the students have recess outside today?
7. What time do you think it is?
8. Why are all the students dressed alike?
9. What time of year is it?
10. What grade level is this classroom of children?

Pictures Tell a Story

Directions: Write answers to the "detective scene" questions below.

1. _____

2. _____

3. _____

4. _____

5. _____

6. _____

7. _____

8. _____

9. _____

10. _____

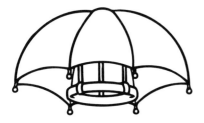

Peculiar Predictions

This activity is a great way to get your students excited about listening to new literature and to encourage them to become active participants during class discussions.

Use a container with an opening large enough for your hand to pass through. An empty square tissue box or a bug catcher toy works great. If you wish, cover the outside of the container with decorative material, paper, or paint. Decorate it with clouds or question marks to create a theme of wonder. Using alphabet stickers, label the container with the title *Peculiar Predictions*.

Select an appropriate book for your students. Preview the book and choose some important people, places, or things that play a special part in the story. Write a word or draw a picture for each noun on a copy of the **Peculiar Predictions Blank Cards reproducible (page 55)**. Make enough cards for your class, cut them out, and place them inside the container.

Have students sit in a circle on the carpet. Then introduce the story title. Explain that inside the special container are several very important words or pictures from the story. Each student's job is to choose a card from the container and make a prediction (guess) about what that card has to do with the story. Pass the container around the circle and have each student choose a card and make a prediction.

When every student has had a chance to give his or her prediction, read the story aloud. Following your reading, discuss with the class whether or not their predictions were confirmed. Repeat the activity with several different books, such as *David's Father* by Robert Munsch. You can use the **Peculiar Predictions Cards reproducibles (pages 53–54)** provided or make cards of your own.

Peculiar Predictions Cards

David's Father by Robert Munsch

spoon

shovel

cheeseburgers

store

girl

bandage

giant

enormous table

Peculiar Predictions Cards

David's Father by Robert Munsch

cars

milkshake

street

snail

boy

father

scraped elbow

tires

Reproducible

Peculiar Predictions Blank Cards

Visualizing

Strategic readers bring the text to life by visualizing it. They engage their senses. They form mental pictures; imagine the sounds, tastes, and smells that are described; and feel the emotions of the characters. By modeling what goes on in your mind as you read, you can enhance young readers' understanding. One of the simplest ways to encourage readers to visualize is to have them draw what they "see in their mind."

Peer Pictures

This activity can be done with a small group or at independent centers. Assign partners and provide students with paper, pencils, crayons, or colored pencils. Ask one student to make up a sentence using descriptive language, for example: *My dog Pepper is black and white.* The richness of detail and description will depend on the ability of the group, so you may wish to provide some ready-made sentences such as the ones listed below. Partners should draw what they see in their minds. Direct partners to compare and discuss their pictures. Have them talk about the words that enabled them to "see" the idea.

Sample Sentences

1. The children hurried into the school when the thunderstorm began.
2. Tom was wearing his new red jacket with gold buttons.
3. My dad just painted our house green with black trim.
4. My little sister has long brown hair and big blue eyes.
5. The short little alien had two long feelers, four fingers on each hand, and only one eye.
6. The big yellow school bus was parked near the playground.

978-1-4129-5824-0

Photo Album

Introduce a new story with this visualization exercise. First, share some family photographs with your students and show them a family picture album. Point out that looking at pictures in an album helps us to remember special times such as holidays, birthdays, and vacations. The pictures remind us who was there, where we were, and what we were doing. Your students may make the connection that their parents often get out the camera and take lots of pictures, too. Explain to students that as they read today's story, they can pretend to take along their own camera. As they read, they can "take pictures" inside their heads. These mental pictures will help them to better understand the story.

After reading together and discussing the story, ask students to describe the images they pictured as they read. Provide each student with a copy of the **Story Photo Album reproducible (page 58)**. Explain that they will create a page for a "photo album" about the characters in the story by drawing the story elements as they saw them pictured in their heads. Share students' visual representations with the class and compile them into a photo album.

Name _____ Date _____

Story Photo Album

Title: _____

Author: _____

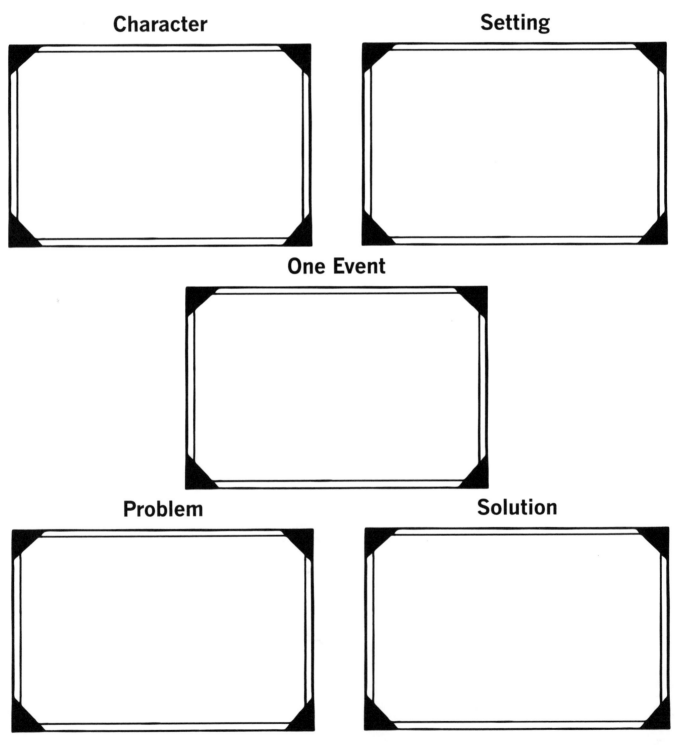

Character

Setting

One Event

Problem

Solution

Questioning

Young children are very inquisitive as they try to make sense of their world. Without being aware of it, children wonder about many things as they look at pictures, listen to conversations, and observe others' facial expressions. Their natural curiosity leads them to ask many questions.

Asking questions is an important strategy that strengthens thinking and enriches the reading experience. Questions help the reader to clarify ideas, giving a clearer picture of the meaning of the text. Wondering about things helps develop children's imaginations. The following activities will encourage children to ask questions before, during, and after reading to enhance their understanding.

Reader's Theater

A Reader's Theater activity offers an engaging means of improving fluency and enhancing comprehension. It blends children's natural desire to perform with the teacher's need to provide oral reading practice. The goal is to enhance reading skills and confidence through practice with a purpose. Reader's Theater gives students a real reason to read aloud, and it motivates reluctant readers.

When introducing the questioning strategy to your students, use the Reader's Theater selection, **Dorothy's Book of Wonders (pages 60–63)**. The script implements the questioning strategy while improving students' understanding of how the strategy works. After using the selection with students, be sure to discuss how Dorothy applied the questioning strategy as she searched for better understanding.

Dorothy's Book of Wonders

Narrator 1: Once upon a time, a young girl named Dorothy walked along the Yellow Brick Road, carrying a special book in her hand.

Narrator 2: Dorothy's *Book of Wonders* was a talking book. Whenever Dorothy had a question, her magical book would tell her the answer.

Narrator 1: Dorothy did not have any idea where she was. She searched through her *Book of Wonders* to help her find her way back home.

Dorothy: Everything looks so beautiful here, but where am I?

Narrator 2: As Dorothy searched, the book began to speak to her.

Wonder Book: You are standing on the Yellow Brick Road.

Narrator 1: Dorothy had to ask more questions to help her get home.

Narrator 2: As she walked, she saw a strange shape in the cornfield.

Dorothy: I wonder what that is?

Narrator 1: Dorothy looked inside her *Book of Wonders* again, hoping to find the answer to her question.

Wonder Book: That is a talking scarecrow.

Narrator 2: Dorothy skipped over to the scarecrow, wondering if he could show her how to get home.

Dorothy's Book of Wonders (cont.)

Dorothy: Excuse me, Scarecrow. Can you help me? I have so many questions! What do I do? Can you help me find my way home?

Scarecrow: I do not have a brain, so I can't help you get home.

Dorothy: Do you know anyone who can help me? And where am I?

Scarecrow: You ask a lot of questions. You must be a good reader, because good readers ask questions.

Dorothy: I am a good reader, but I get confused if I don't ask a lot of questions. I just want to go home to my family. I know they are wondering where I am.

Scarecrow: Let's go find the Tin Man. Maybe he can help you.

Dorothy: Who is the Tin Man?

Scarecrow: You'll see.

Narrator 1: Dorothy did not like the Scarecrow's answer, so she asked her *Book of Wonders* the same question.

Wonder Book: The Tin Man is a man made out of tin.

Dorothy: Well, that didn't help. I will have to keep searching to find out for myself.

Narrator 2: Dorothy and Scarecrow skipped off to see the Tin Man. They hoped he would have all the answers to their questions.

Dorothy's Book of Wonders (cont.)

Scarecrow: There he is. I wonder if he can talk yet.

Dorothy: Why wouldn't he be able to talk? Is he okay?

Scarecrow: He's fine, but he needs some oil to help him talk.

Narrator 1: Dorothy needed to clear up her confusion. She still did not understand why the Tin Man couldn't talk, so she asked again.

Dorothy: Why won't he be able to talk unless he gets some oil?

Scarecrow: He's just a little rusty because no one has talked to him in a long time. Being out in the rain has made him rusty.

Narrator 2: Dorothy was very proud that she had asked her question again, because now she understood why the Tin Man needed oil.

Scarecrow: Hello, Tin Man! Dorothy needs some help. She wants to go home. Can you help her?

Tin Man: Please clarify the question for me. Where is her home?

Narrator 1: Dorothy told Tin Man that she wanted to return to Kansas.

Dorothy: Do you know the way?

Tin Man: I am so excited that you found me. Since you helped me, I am going to help you.

Narrator 2: Dorothy smiled. She couldn't wait to see if all of her good questioning had paid off.

Dorothy's Book of Wonders (cont.)

Tin Man: Oh no! I forgot about Lion. He asked me to bring him dinner. I will have to answer your question later.

Dorothy: Lion? What if he wants to eat us for dinner?

Tin Man: That's a great question, but don't worry. This lion is different. He wouldn't hurt a fly. Here he comes now.

Lion: Where are you going?

Tin Man: We are trying to help Dorothy get home.

Lion: I know how she can get home.

Dorothy: You do? How?

Lion: Click your heels together three times and say, "I wonder, I wonder, I wonder, how I can get home."

Narrator 1: Dorothy wondered how that would work, but she thought she would give it a try. She had run out of questions to ask!

Narrator 2: Dorothy said the words in a loud voice, "I wonder, I wonder, I wonder, how I can get home."

Narrator 1: In that moment, it happened. All of Dorothy's questions paid off. She was back in Kansas with her family!

Dorothy: I used to be scared of asking questions, but now I know how important it is. If I had not asked so many questions, I never would have found my way back home. My *Book of Wonders* and new friends were very helpful!

A Cast of Questions

This questioning game builds students' inferential thinking skills while students gather information. Prior to playing the game, make picture cards showing familiar cartoon characters, foods, animals, and so on. Have students sit in a circle. Choose one student to be the Wizard. The other students must break the Wizard's spell by correctly guessing the identity of the hidden card he or she is holding. To do this, they must ask questions.

Provide a special hat or crown for the Wizard to wear. Pass around a special wand for students to hold when they are the questioner. Once the identity of the card is revealed, the spell has been broken and a new Wizard takes over. When playing the game with younger students, have the Wizard start off with a clue by naming a category in which the word belongs. For example: *The word is a thing.*

Sample Questions

Student 1: *Is it an animal?*

Wizard: *No*

Student 2: *Is it a shape?*

Wizard: *Yes*

Student 3: *Is it a circle?*

Wizard: *No*

Student 4: *Is it a square?*

Wizard: *Yes*

Student 5: *Is it a cartoon character?*

Wizard: *Yes*

Student 6: *Does the character live in the water?*

Wizard: *Yes*

Student 7: *Is it Sponge Bob Square Pants?*

Wizard: *Yes . . . you broke the spell!*

Monitoring and Clarifying

Have you ever read an entire page of a book only to realize that you haven't a clue what you just read? You went through the motions of decoding words but missed the important part of reading—comprehending what you read.

Effective readers ask themselves if what they read makes sense. This strategy is called monitoring and clarifying. Readers use this strategy when they come to a word they do not know, for example. They may try to figure out the word meaning based on the illustrations or context clues. They may also reread or read ahead to clarify.

Building Meaning

A construction worker and a good reader have something in common. A construction worker has a toolbox filled with tools with which to build things, and a good reader has a reading toolbox with which to build meaning. The following tools will help students to monitor and clarify their reading.

Invite students to imagine that they are construction workers while they read. On the job, they come to a sentence that isn't clear because of a "tricky word." They can clarify the sentence by substituting a word that makes sense.

Have a discussion about the ways in which good readers might figure out an unfamiliar word. One method is to read the rest of the sentence and try to find clues to help figure out the word. Another method is to try to make a connection from previous information or experience. Or, students might look for word parts with which they are familiar.

Photocopy and cut out the cards on the **Toolbox Cards reproducibles (pages 67–68)** for this activity. Place the word cards *nervous, sick, happy, sleepy, excited, angry, silly,* and *surprised* in a pocket chart or tape them up where students can see them. These cards will provide a visual aid to help students determine a reasonable answer. Write the following sample sentences on the board.

Sample Sentences

- The little girl was <u>anxious</u> about going to a new school. *(nervous)*
- My <u>ailing</u> dog slept after he ate the garbage. *(sick)*
- I was <u>blissful</u> because I won a trophy. *(happy)*
- I went to bed very late last night, and today I am <u>drowsy</u>. *(sleepy)*
- Tomorrow is my birthday, and I'm <u>eager</u> to open my gifts. *(excited)*
- The dog was <u>annoyed</u> because his bone was missing. *(angry)*
- The clown looked <u>ridiculous</u> when he was standing on his head. *(silly)*
- When Art came home from work, he was <u>shocked</u> to see that the house was clean. *(surprised)*

Read the first sentence with the class and have students replace the underlined word with a more familiar word from the Toolbox Cards. Then discuss how they can apply this same strategy of replacing an unfamiliar word with a familiar one when they are reading a book or other text. Continue with the remaining examples.

The Toolbox Cards can also be used to play a matching game by turning all of the cards facedown in rows of four. The first player turns over two cards to try to find a match. (The pictures on the cards provide clues as to which words match.) If they match, the player keeps them. If not, the player turns them over again. Players take turns until they match all the cards.

Reader's Theater

Use the Reader's Theater selection, **Big, Bad Wolf Returns (pages 69–71)**, to illustrate and reinforce the monitoring and clarifying strategies students should use while reading.

978-1-4129-5824-0

Toolbox Cards

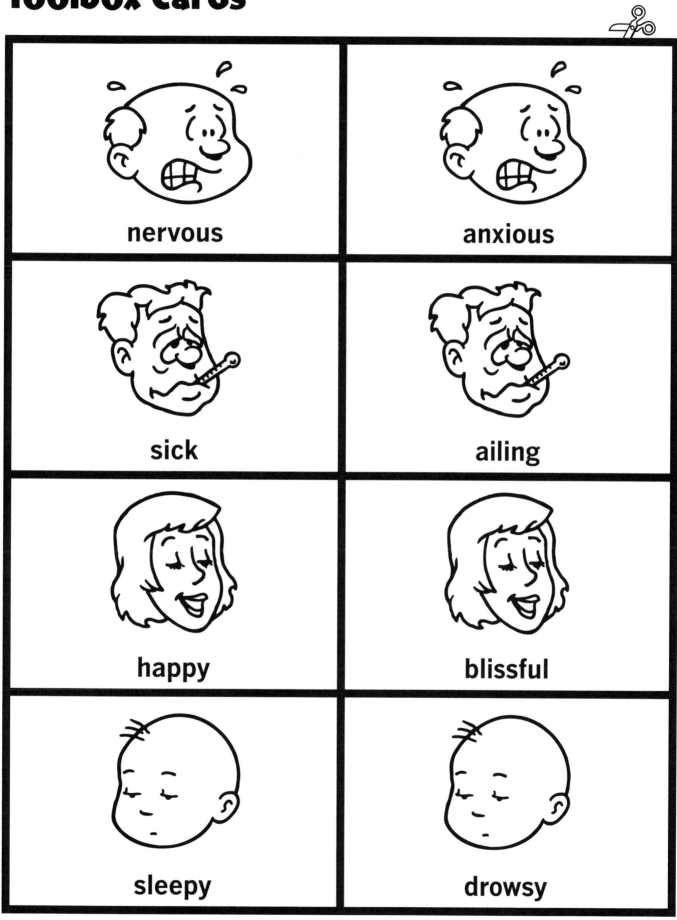

nervous

anxious

sick

ailing

happy

blissful

sleepy

drowsy

Toolbox Cards

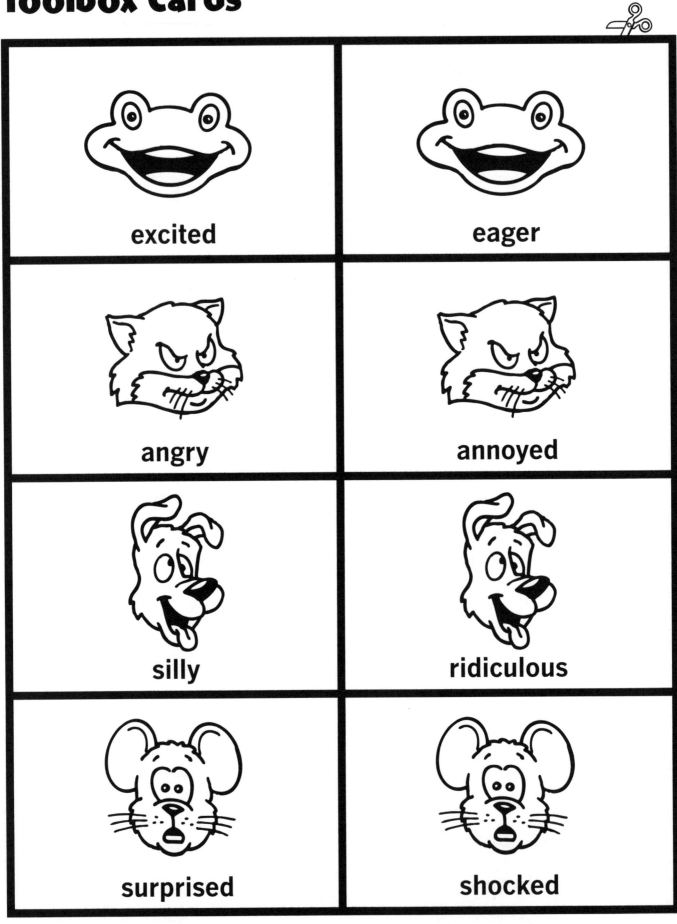

excited

eager

angry

annoyed

silly

ridiculous

surprised

shocked

978-1-4129-5824-0 • © Corwin Press

Name _____ Date _____

Big, Bad Wolf Returns

Narrator 1: It was a beautiful day in Fix-It-Ville, but as always, something was broken.

Narrator 2: Everything in this town seems to break, and only one person knows how to fix it . . . the Wolf.

Wolf: Well, I'm off to fix everyone's mix-ups today.

Narrator 1: Wolf really liked to help people, but he wished that he could just read a book and relax once in awhile.

Narrator 2: One day, Wolf got a phone call from Little Pig.

Wolf: Hello, Mr. Fix-It to the rescue. How can I help you?

Little Pig: Hi, Wolf. This is Little Pig. I really need your help.

Wolf: What is the problem, Little Pig? Is your chair broken?

Little Pig: No, I'm reading a book for Piggy School, and I don't understand some of the story.

Wolf: Were you reading too fast, Little Pig? Sometimes when we read too fast we don't understand the story.

Little Pig: You are right. I was reading too fast. I wanted to finish quickly so I could go outside and play with my friends.

Wolf: Little Pig, you can't be a good reader if you rush through your reading and turn the pages just to get done.

Big, Bad Wolf Returns (cont.)

Little Pig: Thank you for your help, Wolf. I will read more slowly so I understand what I'm reading.

Narrator 1: Wolf was very excited that he helped Little Pig fix her reading problem.

Narrator 2: Wolf had just sat down in his chair when his doorbell rang.

Wolf: What now?

Big Pig: Hi, Mr. Fix-It. This is Big Pig. I need your help.

Wolf: Did your car break down?

Big Pig: No, I was reading a book. I came to a part I didn't understand, so I stopped. I didn't understand the part when the wolf was about to eat the pig. I can't figure out why he would do that.

Wolf: You are really thinking about your reading, Big Pig. Maybe the wolf is hungry and wants to eat a pig for dinner.

Big Pig: How do you know that?

Wolf: Read on. It says right here in this passage, "The wolf was very hungry, so he gobbled up the pig."

Big Pig: You've got to be kidding! Let me read that again. "The wolf was very hungry, so he gobbled up the pig."

Narrator 1: Big Pig now understood. He needed to read on, so the story became clear to him.

Big, Bad Wolf Returns (cont.)

Narrator 2: At last, Wolf sat back down and began reading his book. Just then, the doorbell rang again.

Wolf: Now what?

Smart Pig: Hi, Wolf. I need your help.

Wolf: What's the problem, Smart Pig?

Smart Pig: I can't figure out this tricky word.

Wolf: Did you blend the sounds together?

Smart Pig: I tried that.

Wolf: Did you look for word parts that you know?

Smart Pig: I tried that, too.

Wolf: Did you think of another word that looks like that word?

Smart Pig: Yes, I did all those things, and I still don't know the word.

Wolf: Show me the tricky word. Maybe I can clarify it for you.

Narrator 1: Smart Pig pointed to the word, and Wolf looked confused.

Wolf: Smart Pig, I think you need glasses. You had the book upside down. That's why you didn't know that word!

Narrator 2: Wolf was happy that he had fixed so many problems today. He finally had the chance to sit down, relax, and read his favorite story, *The Three Little Pigs.*

Searching and Selecting

The searching and selecting strategy can be used with many different kinds of text: fiction and nonfiction, textbooks, magazine and newspaper articles, editorials, and much more. Using this strategy, the reader determines what information is important and necessary. In order to do this, the reader needs to set a purpose for reading—for example, to determine the author's opinion or purpose for writing, to define the meaning of a word, to gather information to make a decision, to answer questions, or to solve a problem.

Sifting for Specifics

In this activity, students will listen for important ideas as you read a story to them. Ask if they have ever been to the beach or played in a sandbox. Show them a sand pail, shovel, and sieve. Using a small amount of sand, demonstrate how the sieve works. Explain that a sieve filters out particles or debris from the sand that they might not want when building sand castles. Make the connection that good readers also "sift out the debris," or extra information, when they are reading. Sometimes readers need to determine what information is important and what information is not important.

Read the story *Red Leaf, Yellow Leaf* by Lois Ehlert, and invite students to listen for information about maple trees. Prepare information cards by writing the following sentences on index cards. After reading, display the cards and place them in the sieve. Explain to students that they are going to keep only the important details. Pull out the cards, one by one, and have students determine if each sentence is an important detail to keep. If it is, have a student place the card in the sand pail. If it isn't, place the card in a discard pile. Discuss why the information in the pail is important or necessary to understanding the story and why the other information does not affect understanding. Emphasize to students that as they read or listen to books, they need to sift out the less important parts of the story or the information that is not helpful in answering their questions.

Information Cards for Red Leaf, Yellow Leaf

- The girl loves her tree.
- The wind can scatter seeds, and trees can grow anywhere.
- Sometimes squirrels eat the seeds.
- Seeds can sprout in the spring when the sun shines on them.
- Trees are happy.
- A man came into the woods and collected the tree sprouts.
- The birds built nests in the tree.
- A hole must be dug to plant a tree.
- People buy trees in a garden center.
- Leaves get their green color from chlorophyll.
- Tiny leaves form from buds on the trees.
- We can make maple syrup from the sap collected from maple trees.
- Bark is the outer skin of a tree.

Clean Up the Clutter

This activity is another way to help students understand that when readers search and select, they look for necessary and important ideas. Ask students if they have ever helped around the house by picking up or cleaning their rooms. Maybe they have helped reorganize a closet or clean out the garage. Sometimes there is so much stuff that some items must be thrown away. When people are cleaning up at home, they might put their things into three piles: things to save, things to throw away, and things they might use later. As good readers read, they make the same choices. They decide what information they should keep, what information they can ignore or "throw away," and what information they might need later.

Prepare story cards for *Amazing Grace* by Mary Hoffman, using following the sentences. Write each sentence on an index card. Read the story together and have students look for information and identify the story elements. Write the following headings on chart paper: *Information to: Keep, Throw Away,* and *Maybe Use.*

Read the index cards one at a time with students. Encourage discussion and let students decide in which category to place each story card. There are no right or wrong answers when placing the cards, as long as students can explain why they have chosen the particular categories.

Story Cards for Amazing Grace

- Grace loved stories.
- Grace loved to act out all the parts of a story.
- Grace lived with her grandmother, or Nana, and mother.
- The teacher said the class would perform the play *Peter Pan.*
- The other kids said Grace could not be Peter Pan.
- Grace's mother said that Grace could be anything she wanted to be.
- Nana's friend lived in Trinidad.
- Raj was chosen to play the part of Captain Hook.
- Grace practiced and practiced for the audition.
- Grace was fantastic when she tried out for the part of Peter Pan.
- Everyone voted for Grace to be Peter Pan.
- Everyone thought the play was wonderful.
- If someone perseveres or keeps trying, she can do anything she wants.

Summarizing

One of the joys of reading is the conversation that ensues and the sharing that occurs when we have enjoyed a good book. Summarizing is a part of the conversation. Teaching students to summarize will empower them to comprehend at a deeper level. Through dialogue with others, readers strengthen their own understanding. The following activities are designed to make students aware of a story's events, sequence, and elements. Use the **Comprehension Strategy Cards (pages 76–78)** to guide student discussion. Cut out, laminate, and hole-punch several sets of cards and place them on a ring. The rings provide a great way for students to monitor their own reading when they read independently.

Star Summary

This activity can be done in any setting, whether you are reading aloud to students or working in small groups. After students practice, they can try it as they read with a partner or independently. The idea is simply to teach them to identify story elements.

Ask students if they have a favorite TV star, character, singer, or athlete. What other famous people do they know of? People are often interested in someone who is popular or famous. They may read about them or watch stories about them. Some famous people are often called "stars."

Explain to students that in a story, one character is usually the star, or the most important character. As the story unfolds, we learn more about the star, for example, what problems he has, what happens as he tries to solve his problems, and what he is thinking or feeling. The star may be a person or an animal. After we read, we want to try and remember special things about the star character.

On chart paper or the board, draw a large star. Label the points with the headings *Setting, Problem, Event, Solution,* and *Feelings or Actions.* In the center of the star, write the star character's name. Call on students to help you fill in the main points of the star. For younger students, have sentence strips prepared with the story elements written on them. Ask students to decide on which point of the star they would place each strip. Emphasize that these main points, or important ideas, are what readers use to summarize the story. Then use the main points to retell the story. You can also have students fill in their own copies of the **Star Summary reproducible (page 79)**.

Comprehension Strategy Cards

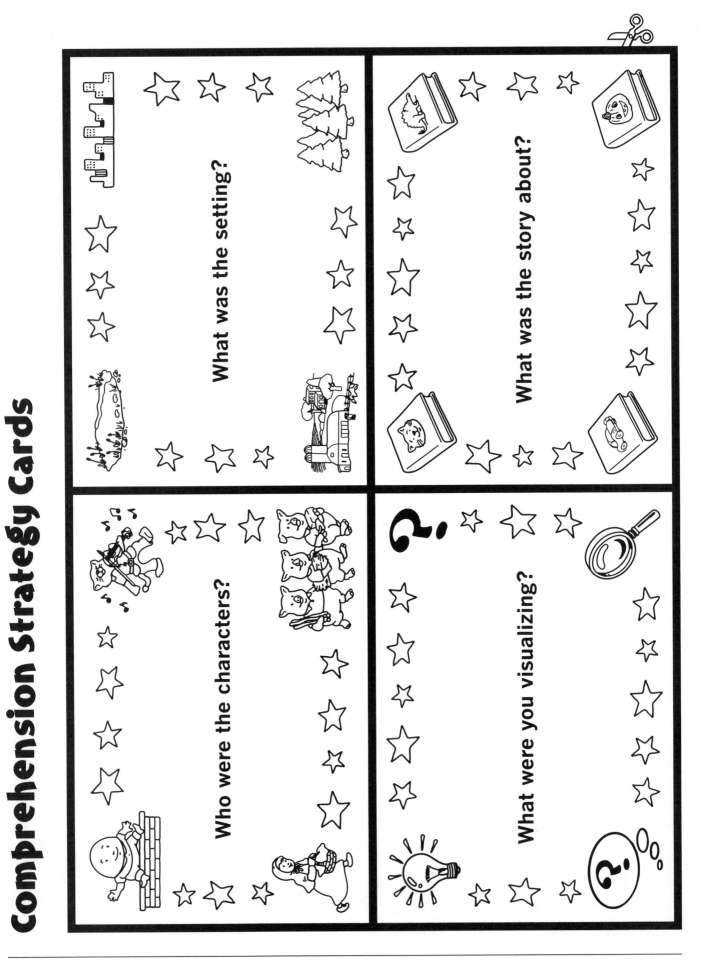

What was the setting?

What was the story about?

Who were the characters?

What were you visualizing?

978-1-4129-5824-0 • © Corwin Press

Comprehension Strategy Cards

What is the illustrator's job?

What did the story remind you of?

Did the pictures tell you more about the story?

What is the author's job?

Comprehension Strategy Cards

Do you have any questions?

Does this remind you of another story?

How did the story make you feel? Why?

What were you thinking about?

Reproducible   978-1-4129-5824-0 • © Corwin Press

Name _____ Date _____

Star Summary

Title: _____

Author: _____

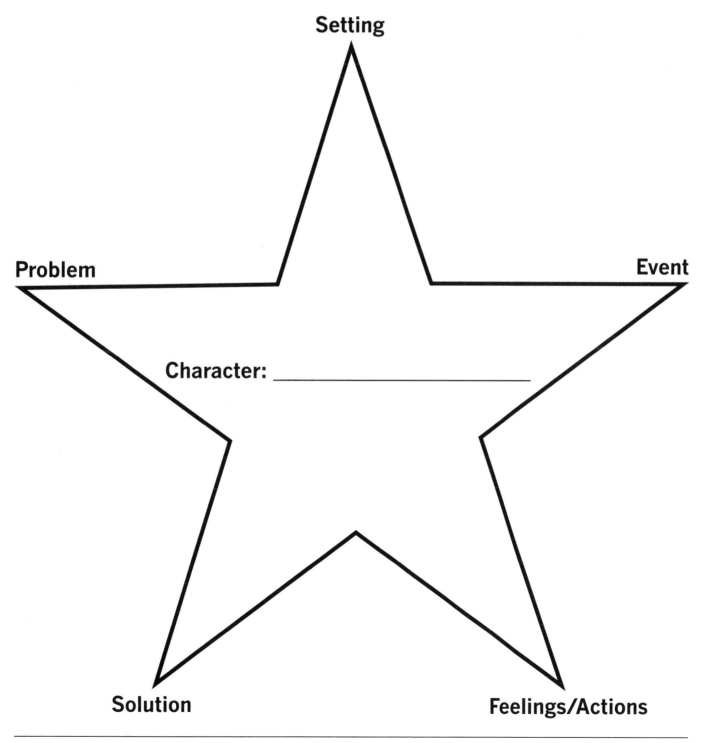

Setting

Problem

Event

Character: _____

Solution

Feelings/Actions

Cut It Down to Size and Summarize

Writing a summary can be a difficult task for some students because they tend to include too much information. In this activity, show students that with just a few words, they can recognize a favorite nursery rhyme or story. Using the "Somebody wanted . . . But . . . So then . . ." summary format or a story element graphic organizer, students can quickly summarize a story.

Tell students that you will give them some clues about a story. Can they correctly guess the story from the clues?

Somebody wanted . . . But . . . So then . . .

1. A pig comes to visit, and a girl feeds her a pancake. One thing leads to another. *(If You Give a Pig a Pancake)*
2. A small bear in a department store waits to be purchased, but no one wants him because he has a button missing. So he goes off to search for his lost button. *(Paddington)*

Story Element Graphic Organizer

Characters	Setting	Problem	Solution
pigs/wolf	straw/stick house	house blown down	brick house
girl/wolf	woods	hungry wolf	hunter
spider	waterspout	washed out	sun came out
egg	wall	fell down	king's men

After students have correctly identified the story or nursery rhyme, reinforce that summaries are short and to the point and do not tell every detail of the story. Make this activity ongoing throughout the school year. Use your favorite class read-aloud books and quiz students about the stories they have heard.

978-1-4129-5824-0

Storyboard

This whole-class activity invites students to summarize the elements of a story. This example is based on the story *David's Father* by Robert Munsch. Photocopy the **Storyboard Cards reproducibles (pages 82–83)** and cut out the cards.

On the board or chart paper, write the following headings: *Characters*, *Setting*, *Problem*, and *Solution*. Read the story aloud to the class. When the story is completed, read the Storyboard Cards to the class. Call on students to identify to which story element each card refers. Place the cards in the correct categories. Then use the cards to make an oral or written summary of the story.

Storyboard Cards: Character and Setting

David's Father by Robert Munsch

Julie	David	grandmother
three men	giant	storekeeper
store	kitchen	bedroom
David's house	middle of the sidewalk	walking home from school

Reproducible

Storyboard Cards: Problem and Solution

David's Father by Robert Munsch

The big kids took the ice cream.	David's father said, "These kids are my friends."	Julie didn't like the food that David's father offered her.	Julie hid in her room.
David's father put a bandage on her elbow.	The storekeeper would not help the kids.	David's father yelled, "Stop!"	Julie was afraid of her new neighbors.
Julie hurt her elbow.	David's father yelled, "Beat it!"	David and Julie could not cross the street.	Julie had a second milkshake instead.

CHAPTER 3

Put Your Hats in Order

Graphic Organizers

A graphic organizer is a visual aid used to help students organize information. It allows them to further develop comprehension and foster understanding in a fun and engaging way. It is a tool for beginning readers to develop reading strategies as they explore various concepts and helps them to focus on key points while thinking and writing.

Graphic organizers come in many different forms, each one best suited to organize a particular type of information. They have been widely researched for their effectiveness in improving learning outcomes for a variety of learners.

There are many different ways to use the graphic organizers provided in this book. Adapt them for any grade level and ability group. First, model the use of a graphic organizer. Then give students a shared experience to ensure that they understand how to effectively use each organizer.

Finally, the graphic organizers can be used as tools for students to independently monitor their understanding of a text and to keep track of and organize their thoughts.

My KWL Chart

I **K**now . . .	I **W**ant to Know . . .	I **L**earned . . .

Name _____ Date _____

World of Prior Knowledge

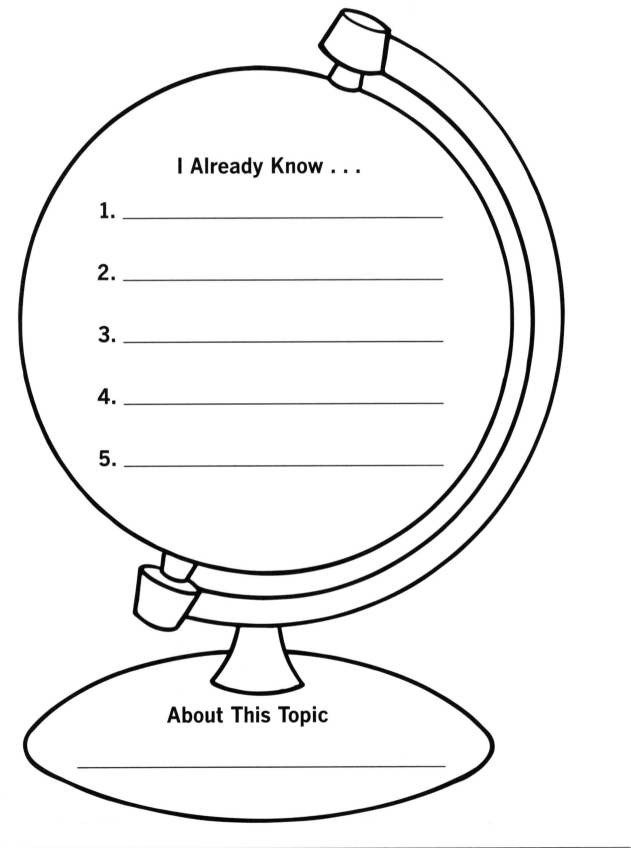

I Already Know . . .

1. _____

2. _____

3. _____

4. _____

5. _____

About This Topic

_____

Name _____ Date _____

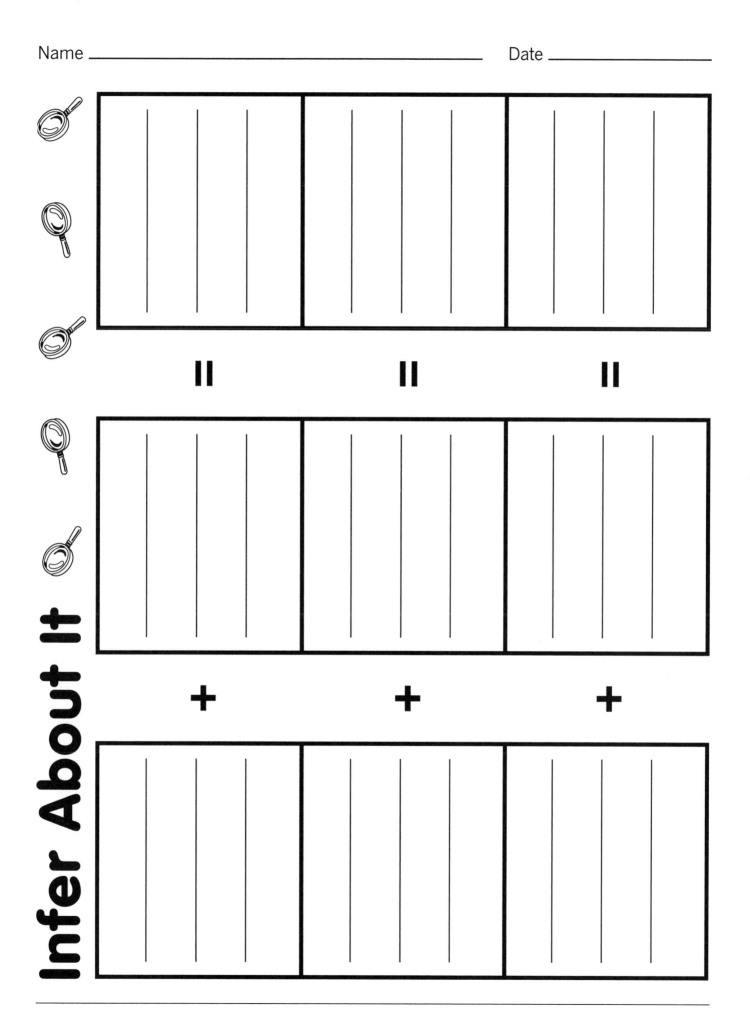

Name _____ Date _____

Predict It!

Directions: Make your prediction and color the star if it comes true!

My prediction based on the title and cover.

My prediction for what I will learn.

Reproducible   978-1-4129-5824-0 • © Corwin Press

Name _____ Date _____

Drift Off

My thoughts drifted off
While reading today.
My mind formed a picture
As if out of clay!

First, I visualized . . .

Then, I visualized . . .

Just the Facts

Who?

What?

When?

Where?

Why?

Name _____   Date _____

Fact Finder

Name _____   Date _____

A Mess of Information

This does not make sense to me . . .

_____

_____

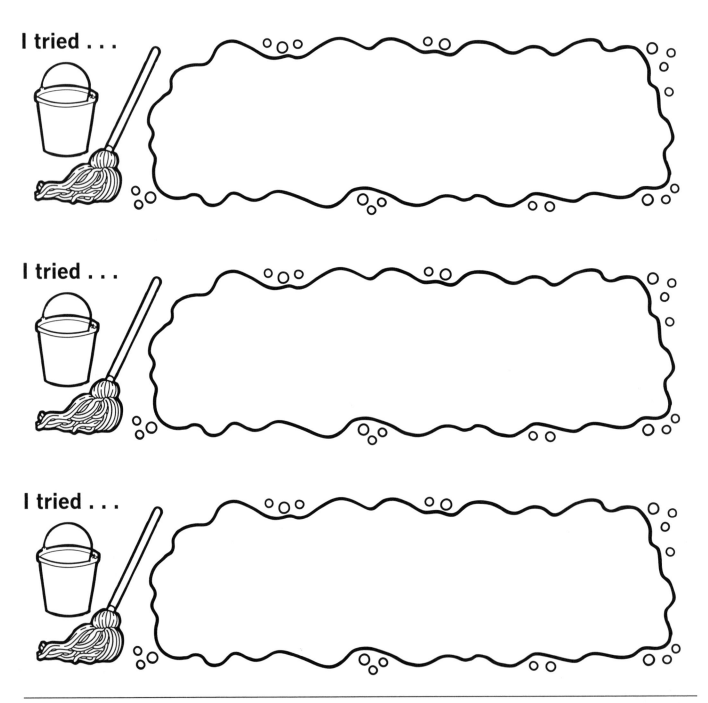

I tried . . .

I tried . . .

I tried . . .

Reproducible

Name _____   Date _____

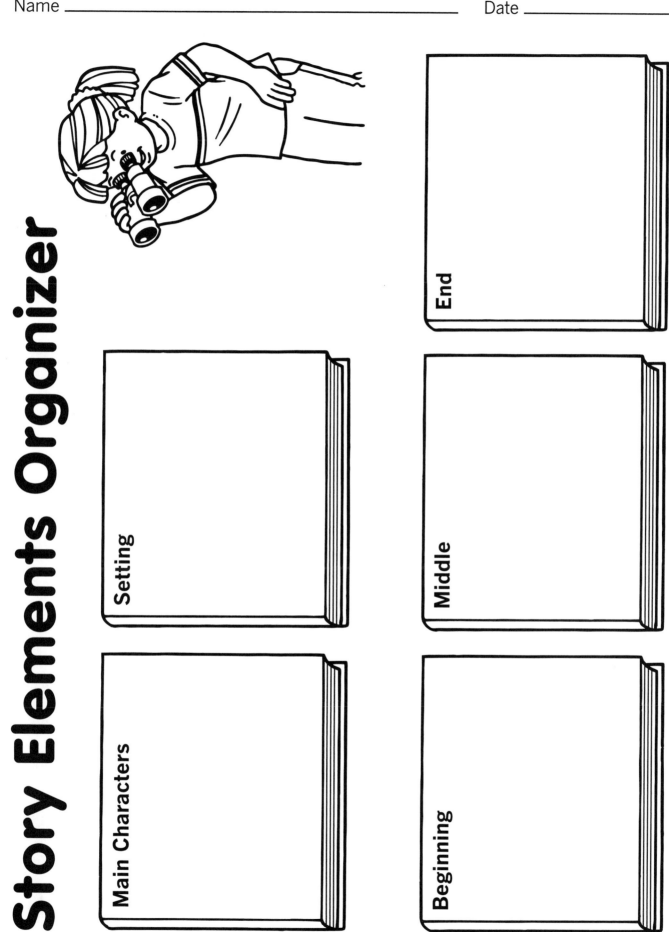

Story Elements Organizer

Main Characters

Setting

Beginning

Middle

End

Name _____ Date _____

Story Elements House

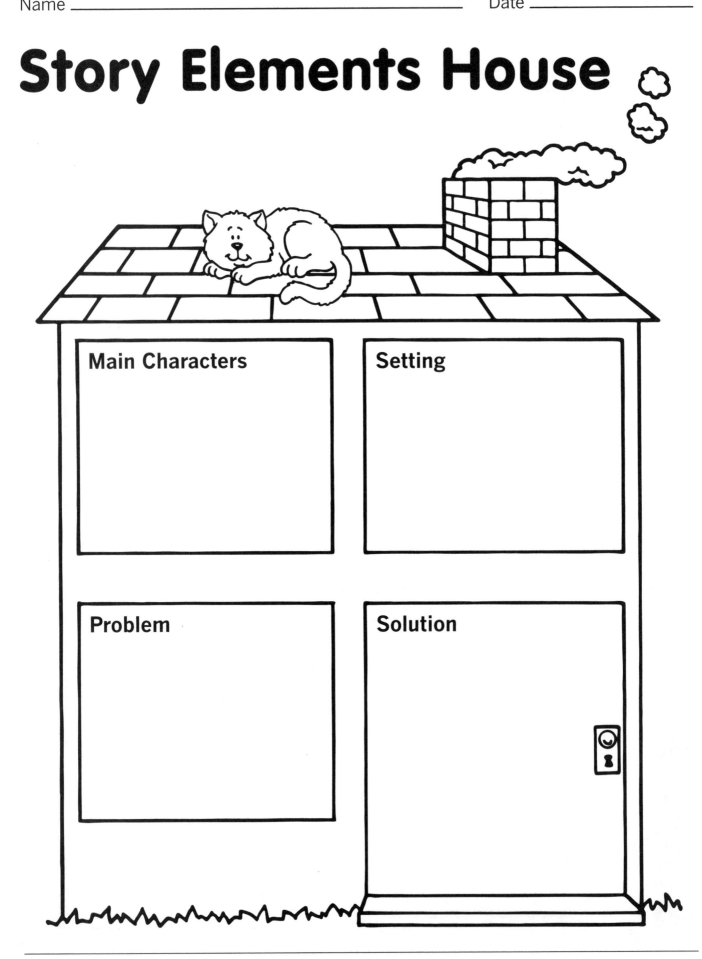

Main Characters

Setting

Problem

Solution

Reproducible

Name _____   Date _____

Same But Different

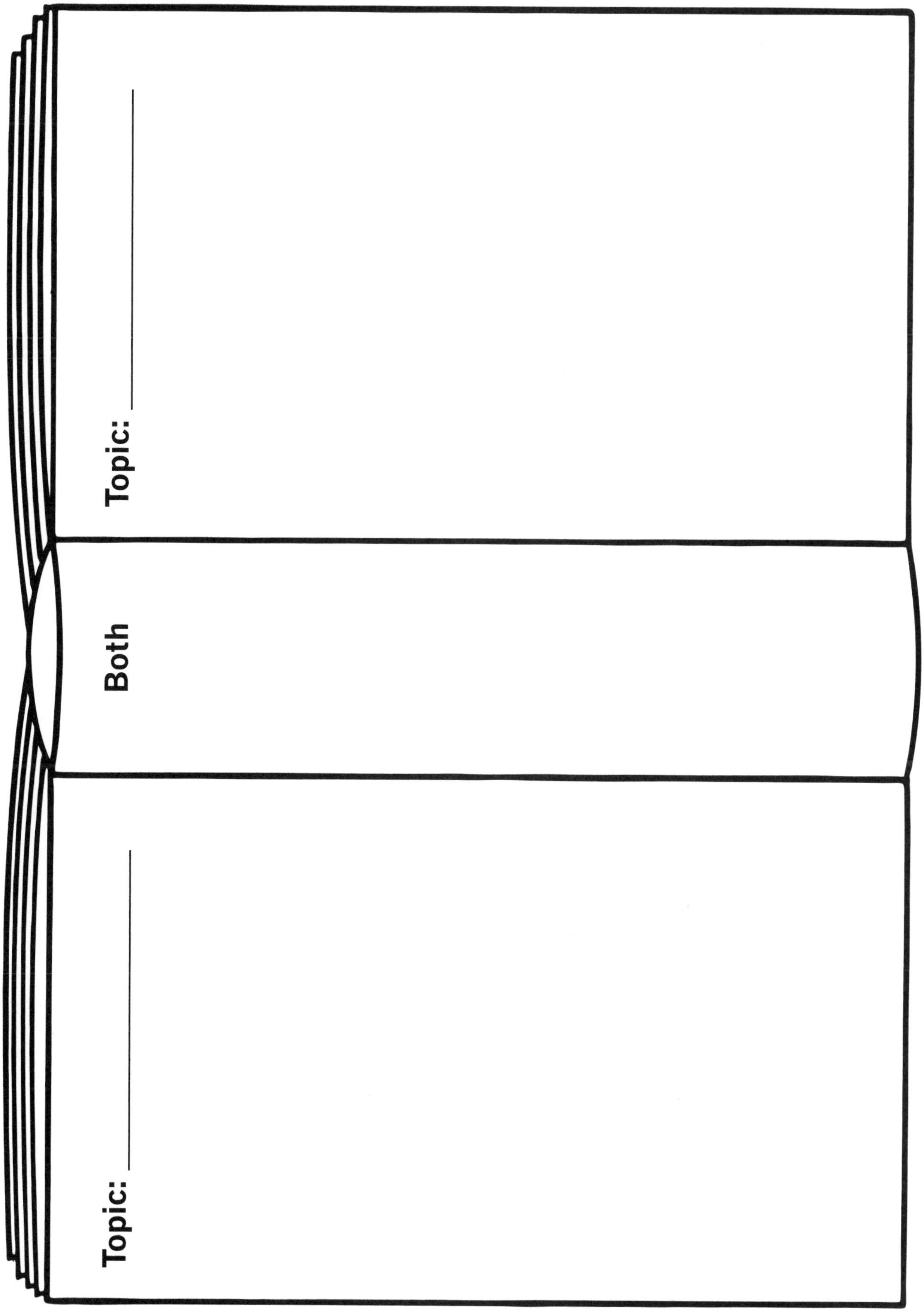

Topic: _____

Both

Topic: _____

References

Brown, A. L., & Day, J. D. (1983). Macrorules for summarizing texts: The development of expertise. *Journal of Verbal Learning and Verbal Behavior, 22,* 1–14.

Brown, A. L., Day, J. D., & Jones, R. S. (1983). The development of plans for summarizing texts. *Child Development, 54,* 968–979.

Ehlert, L. (1991). *Red leaf, yellow leaf.* San Diego, CA: Harcourt Brace and Company.

Hall, S. (2006). *I've dibel'd, now what?* Longmont, CO: Sopris West Educational Services.

Harvey, S., & Gouduis, A. (2000). *Strategies that work.* Markham, Ontario: Pembroke Publishers Limited.

Hoffman, M. (1991). *Amazing Grace.* New York, NY: Scholastic.

Hoyt, L. (1999). *Revisit, reflect, retell.* Portsmouth, NH: Heinemann.

Jones, B. F., Pierce, J., & Hunter, B. (1988/1989). Teaching students to construct graphic representations. *Educational Leadership, 46*(4), 20–25.

Lobel, A. (1970). *Frog and Toad are friends.* New York, NY: HarperCollins Publishers, Inc.

McEwan, E. K. (2002). *Teach them all to read: Catching the kids who fall through the cracks.* Thousand Oaks, CA: Corwin Press.

Munsch, R. (1993). *David's father.* Toronto, Ontario: Annick Press Limited.

Shankweiler, D., Lundquist, E., Katz, L., Stuebing, K. K., Fletcher, J. M., Brady, S., Fowler, A., Dreyer, L. G., Marchione, K. E., Shaywitz, S. E., & Shaywitz, B. A. (1999). Comprehension and decoding: Patterns of association in children with reading difficulties. *Scientific Studies of Reading, 3*(1), 69–94.

Zimmermann, S., & Hutchins, C. (2003). *Seven keys to comprehension.* New York, NY: Three Rivers Press.

978-1-4129-5824-0